Copyright @Harare Streets Publishing 2023

Published by Harare Streets Publishing

TOWNSHIP BOYS

A Unique Anthology of Zimbabwean Township Histories

TABLE OF CONTENTS

Chapter One: Introducing the Pre-Independence Township – ....
By Chester Mhende 8
Chapter Two: Furtherance ....
By Frank Lupafya 19
Chapter Three: "Saints" ....
By Tapera Knox Chitiyo.. 29
Chapter Four: The Making of Canderton Infrastructure Group ....
By Derek Zhanje... 53
Chapter 5: Seke
By Munyukwi Milton Kahari 69
Chapter Six: The Zimbabwe Dream ....
By Tafi Chihota 93
Chapter 7: Township Life vs. Afrikan Identity ....
By Unathi Mbolekwa (Nyathi) 109
Chapter Eight: Township Music- My First Love! ....
By John Matinde... 130
Chapter Nine: Ghetto Short Stories
By Richard Tanyanyiwa 159
Chapter Ten: From the Village to the City via War ....
By Masimba Charles Chiganze 178
Chapter Eleven: The Kingdom Man..
By Nigel Chanakira 216

Make a smart move with **Shelter!**

Shelter Zimbabwe

Projects on Offer

Rockview Park 1E
situated along Mutare road next to Sunway
1000sqm – **$30,000.00**

Adelaide Park
situated along Mutare road next to Rockview Park 1E
300sq – **$16,000.00**

Mabvuku Chizhanje
situated along Mutare road between Old Tafara & Zimre
Price **$11,500.00**

Marondera Lendy Park
sited next to Lendy park primary along first 1200sqm
Price **$27,500.00**

With flexible payment terms up to 24 months to pay and 2**0% deposit**

 0719 551 234   95 Fife Avenue   www.shelter.co.zw

Shelter Zimbabwe
Your Destination for a Secure Future!

0719 551 234   95 Fife Avenue
www.shelter.co.zw

Author Biographies

Chester Mhende is an established businessman and politician.

Qabaniso Lupafya considers himself as just your average Zimbabwean.

Dr Knox Tapera Chitiyo is born and raised in Zimbabwe. He is a Senior Associate Fellow at Chatham House and is also President of the Britain Zimbabwe Society.

Derek Zhanje lives by the saying: "No retreat no surrender-backwards never, forward forever by ginya!!!

Milton Kahari is and International Business Management Professional with an Engineering undergraduate degree, an MBA and several certificates.

Tafi Chihota went to the University of Redlands, San Bernardino, CA, USA and is self-employed and living in Harare. He is a devoted family man and pan-Africanist.

Unathi Mbolekwa (Nyathi) Is a Pan-Africanist and intellectual.

Jon Matinde is a pop news pundit but all together music. He's helped found a few radio stations. He's a broadcast and media practitioner and a TV and radio trainer.

Richard Tanyanyiwa is born and bred in Mbare and very proud, passionate and unapologetic about his roots!

Masimba Chiganze was born in 1960 in rural Rusape. At 15, while at a mission boarding school, he joined the liberation war in Mozambique and ended up studying aviation in Ethiopia

Nigel Chanakira is an economist by training, an investment banker by profession, a businessman by choice and a success coach and facilitator by passion.

Chapter One: Introducing the Pre-Independence Township –

By Chester Mhende

I was born Chester Nhamo Mhende on 13 June 1957 at Harare Hospital (ku Gomo) while my parents resided at 22 Mukarati Street, Mufakose, Salisbury.

We would later move to stay with my maternal uncle Mr. James Muzhuzha Nyatsambo in Beatrice Cottages; then National Township; and then to my aunt in Western Triangle (Cherima), Highfields.

My father was a teacher and then became a farm manager at Bourtonvale farm (Chivere) in Mrepatepa, Bindura

As a youth in Harare, I have vivid memories of several things starting as a little boy playing chabuta (coin game) to raise pocket money to supplement money which would buy buns and milk to eat while on break at school.

In later years I lived with my maternal aunt who had a house in Cherima. We would ride a bus at 07.15 every morning just off present-day Glen Norah police station to my aunt's workplace on a Salisbury United Omnibus. Once in the city we would drop off at the Charge Office (main police station in town) at 07.45, in time to start work at Roan Stationery, which was corner Angwa street and Railway Ave (present day T M

Supermarket), with the opposite end of the building (corner Angwa with South Ave) being the Customs building.

The other side of the street was George Elcombe town office with the railway station across the road.

I have fond memories of our journeys to Bulawayo by train. You booked your coach by number with second class taking two people, with clean bedding provided and the dining room providing a three-course dinner, and warm water in the public toilet down the passage.

What was vivid when we came to town was how most black people were messengers on bicycles, drivers, and tea boys with most office work reserved for white people despite that some of the whites were not so clever.

In our day back in the township, we bought milk in a one-litre bottle from the then Salisbury Dairibord Company with tokens that you placed inside the bottle and left the empty bottle with the token by the gate.

When the milkman came, he would religiously replace the empty bottle with a full one and take the token as his payment.

The token held the street value of the milk.

In those days milk and coke were bought only if you had an empty bottle to exchange.

As money was an issue, we would walk from Cherima to Machipisa where my good friends Israel Chirata and Dzinesu Mbofana lived with their parents and siblings.

Often, I would walk further to National to visit my paternal uncle who often would be at Mbare Musika where he had his mukambo table (he sold used clothing that he bought from white people in the suburbs -white only areas).

In those days, black people lived in the black-only townships of Mufakose, Highfields, Glen Norah, Kambuzuma, Gillingham (now Dzivaresekwa), Parkridge (now Warren hills into Kuwadzana), with Mabvuku and Tafara being the main township for maids and gardeners. Single men were not allowed female visitors and consequently they stayed in the *Magaba* and *Matapi* hostels bordering Mbare Musika.

If you had a wife and children they had to stay in the villages in the rural areas, and they needed a permit from their local police station in the village to visit town. They would come to town mainly to collect money from their husbands in town for medication, school fees or for medical attention at 'Gomo' (Harare Hospital).

I remember my uncle going to present day *Mbudzi* to give his wife money at 7 miles hotel then she rode the next bus back to their village in Mhondoro.

Coloured people lived in Southerton, Ardbennie, St Martins and Arcadia.

Indians lived in Kopje, Ridgeview, Lincoln Green, and part of Belvedere along Jameson Ave (now Samora Machel).

White people had the luxury of most of the northern suburbs, (anywhere north of Jameson Avenue from Belvedere, Milton

Park, Avondale, Avonlea, Mount Pleasant, Emerald Hill, Marlborough, Newlands, Highlands, Borrowdale, Eastlea, Greendale and later Gun Hill). A sprinkling of the poorer whites were mixed with well to do coloured peopled in Braeside and Cranborne, Hillside and Hatfield. These poor whites were mainly mechanics and truck drivers driving for the National Railways lorries and trains, commonly referred to as Goods trains.

For entertainment, blacks mainly met at Mushandira Pamwe at Machipisa and Skyline motel as Salisbury town was the preserve of white people.

It was at these places that we all congregated every day after work, on Saturdays and Sundays for drinks, networking while Thomas Mapfumo, Safirio Madzikatire, Oliver Mutukudzi and other artists performed their lovely songs which kept us entertained.

The other forms of entertainment were movies at Rainbow, Kambuzuma, and Liberty cinema in Cameron Street or soccer on Sundays at Gwanzura stadium in Machipisa, Highfields or Rufaro stadium in Mbare.

I remember in those days, National had public speakers alongside streetlights. The speakers would amplify the voice of a white man who would announce the arrival of a black person from the villages, or a lost child and this would allow relatives of the announced people to know they had a visitor or a lost family member, and resultantly, they would collect their relatives from Mbare or Matapi police stations.

In those days, a black man needed a permit to drink clear beer.

Blacks drank Rufaro 'mhamba' which was a sorghum based alcoholic drink served at council bars in 1-litre plastic containers which we would shake and share the drink by handing the container from one person to the next.

Later, a brewery was opened in Chitungwiza for a more sorghum based alcoholic beverage which was not allowed to be sold in the Salisbury townships, and thus was only sold in the newly established Chitungwiza dormitory town and villages.

Clear beer was the preserve of white people at that time, and later, only upper class black people like bus operators, supermarket owners, lecturers and big policemen drank 'clear beer'.

In earlier years, black people were not allowed into the city centre on First Street, unless they worked in city. Even then, a black person had to step off the pavement if there was a white man walking on the pavement in the black man's direction.

In those days blacks would be found around Charge Office (which was the main bus station in town centre) and later another bus station was built at Market Square as the population increased.

I had an aunt who was a maid in Greendale, and when we went to visit her, we needed a permit to ride on the bus with white people.

In those days, public transport was reliable, affordable and on time, whether you were riding a local town bus or riding a bus to the village. It didn't matter whether the bus was town or rural based because the system was efficient.

Roads were lit up, without potholes, and cars could drive at high speeds without the danger of potholes.

Streets were clearly marked with lanes.

I saw potholes for the first time in the city centre of Lusaka, Zambia in 1979 when I visited my paternal uncle and his family.

To make that journey, because of sanctions that were imposed on Rhodesia at the time, I flew into Zambia from Francistown in Botswana.

I used to think Zambian drivers were drunkards as they never drove straight because of potholes on 'Cairo Road' which was the main road in town centre… not realizing that they were avoiding potholes.

In 1964 Zambia had achieved independence becoming a black independent state formerly, Northern Rhodesia while current day Zimbabwe was Southern Rhodesia.

I was one of the first few black people to move into white areas when a white man was brave enough, (probably forced by lack of demand) to rent me his house in Emerald Hill in 1978.

This was because white population numbers were decreasing, as many were losing their lives in the liberation war against the black liberation fighters (referred to by whites as terrorists (terrs) or guerillas - likened to animals).

Once legalized, in 1979, I bought my first house in Greystone Park on a mortgage from CABS where I paid $26.50 a month to service my debt.

I would sell that house in 1986 for $36,750 to buy my present house (which was very expensive then) for $65,000.

Black Independence came in 1980.

The transition of Rhodesia to Zimbabwe occurred in the year 1979 into 1980 when black majority rule was fulfilled. That was very eventful.

I remember blacks in villages being confined to KEEPs. KEEPs were fenced off holding areas designed to hold villagers to prevent the villagers mixing with the liberation heroes (terrs). The whites did not want them mixing with the liberation heroes affectionately known as "the boys" who were slowly integrating into society.

The whites feared that "the boys" would influence villagers to vote for the Zimbabwe African National Union (ZANU), the liberation movement led by Robert Gabriel Mugabe, which they viewed as communist. Instead the whites preferred their puppet party in the form of the United African National Council (UANC) led by Bishop Abel Muzorewa

Unfortunately for them, the black man had identified a common enemy in anything white or anything that was associated with whites. As a result of this Black Nationalist solidarity, ZANU won decisively in 1980, much to the dismay of the whites.

Eventually, the curated Lancaster House peace agreement ushered in Independence.

The Lancaster agreement reserved 20 percent of parliament and cabinet ministerial posts to whites for a 5-year transition so that white interests would be protected; with the army led by a white General Peter Walls, the ministry of Finance led by a white minister David Smith, and the agriculture ministry assigned to Dennis Norman.

Independence saw massive rural to urban migration as people moved to town in search for better life, as this was the key promise of the struggle.

This saw utilities (roads, buses, water, sewer, electricity) gradually come under stress as the Salisbury infrastructure was designed for a limited few- a population number way below one million inhabitants.

As buses came under pressure, the Zimbabwean government introduced rural bus owners, ferrying people from the rural to urban areas through the Zimbabwe Road Motor Transport led by Mr. Ben Mucheche and Mr. Solomon Tawengwa. It incorporated most rural bus operators.

That would soon fail, as the concept of cooperatives that were owned by many was alien to them, and thus wrangles became the order of the day resultantly affecting efficiency of services.

That was followed by the introduction of kombis (little microbuses) carrying initially 8 passengers, but eventually kombis would carry 18 to 20 passengers at a time. These too, could not cope and that saw cars- mainly station wagons- join the fray of the transport business until ultimately the bottom collapsed. In the present day we have the 'mishikashika' which are small Japanese cars acting as informal taxis to tansport people.

This has led to congestion, unruly drivers, road rage and increasing accidents as most of those "mishikashika" vehicles are poorly maintained, and the law cannot cope with the increase in number of the informal vehicles. The police are poorly paid, and corruption has become the order of the day while potholes are rampant and road carnage escalates.

With the influx of people into the towns and cities, the township reticulation system could not cope with water demand resulting in tap water not being good enough for human consumption. This was exacerbated by the excessive demand leading to leakages and breakages of water pipes. A lot of purified water was lost on the way from the treatment plant to city residents. Furthermore, the treatment chemicals became expensive and this was an additional issue.

April 18 1980… independence arrived in Zimbabwe in a dramatic fashion, movie style!

I remember the then guerilla leader, comrade Robert Mugabe arriving aboard helicopter into Zimbabwe grounds. He was flanked by our war heroes, the likes of comrade Solomon

Mujuru whose nom de guerre was Rex Nhongo. The people in Zimbabwe Grounds erupted into a frenzy. Most people could not believe that they were truly witnessing Liberation in the making! Elections followed and the Liberation movement of ZANU Patriotic Front (PF) romped to victory to everyone's delight.

In those days, the economy functioned well, the cities were well administered, and life was generally good. Today, 43 years later, cities are now overcrowded which is the result of rural to urban migration.

Today, the nation is heavily polarized, and lawlessness is the order of the day.

Small examples of lawlessness include our traffic jungle where you find single file of four lanes in one direction on a road designated for one lane!

Nightmares include people being arrested and staying in remand for extended periods before trial or languishing without trial.

Also today, money is an issue. As I write, the country is operating in a multi-currency environment with inflation running very high at around 100 percent per annum! It was not the same in the pre-independent period; neither was it like this in the 1980s or 1990s.

As I write this, the bank-lending interest rates are at 200 percent to control inflation and regulate the currency fall. The economy is in dire straits. In fact, the economy is on a banana skin as prices are beyond the reach of many, while unemployment is rampant, estimated at around 90 percent of the adult population!

Former President Mugabe did a very good job of lifting black man's esteem through Land Reform and Indigenization policies which empowered blacks, improved education which widened our horizons and gave way into formal employment.

Chapter Two: Furtherance

By Frank Lupafya

My name is Qabaniso Frank Lupafya. I was born on June 21st, 1968, near Chinhoyi (formerly called Sinoia) at a place called Alaska Mine. My father, Frank Cripps Lupafya moved from South Africa to Zimbabwe (formerly Rhodesia) in the late 1950s (or perhaps early 1960s- I'm not sure of the exact dates). My mother is Rachel Elizabeth Lupafya, who grew up in the Harare township of Highfields. My parents met when my mother was at Alaska Mine on holiday visiting her uncle.

My father was born in Messina, South Africa on the 28th of November 1940. My late father was an amazing man. He was fluent in more than eight languages, including Zulu, Venda, Xhosa, Ndebele, Shona, Nyanja, Bemba, Afrikaans, English and Flemish. He also spoke multiple regional dialects from Malawi, Zambia, Botswana, Zimbabwe, Mozambique, and Belgium and of course South Africa. He came to Zimbabwe as a personal assistant ("Teaboy") for his Afrikaner boss who had been transferred to Alaska Mine from Messina. My father initially worked as a 'Teaboy' (a job that entailed serving tea to his white bosses). He constantly self-developed to eventually start his own successful businesses, which he operated until he passed away in 2009.

We lived at Alaska Mine for the first few years of my life. My father then started his career as a salesman for Rothman's

Cigarette Company and we moved to Chinhoyi. Dad was promoted to be a lead salesman in Bulawayo. Remember the old man spoke many languages and his employers recognized that unique skill set. He was able to increase sales for Rothmans to some remote areas where they had not been able to access. His multilingual skills and his electric personality catapulted success trajectory in the corporate world. Along with my dad's success came a better quality of life for our family. I recall back in the early 70s my mother got her driver's license. It was extremely progressive of my parents to do that at the time, because it was generally unheard of for a black woman in white Rhodesia to be driving back then.

Pause!!!

Pre-independence in the late 1970s, the Lupafya family lived in Glen Norah. I spent my childhood in Harare (formerly Salisbury). Glen Norah was one of the Townships created by white-ruled Rhodesia. These townships were established to be separate living areas for blacks, while the whites lived in more affluent suburbs. The white population at the time was less than 10% of the entire population; but controlled 95% of the wealth and 100% of the power. No whites lived in the townships, and no blacks lived in the suburbs. Before independence, white children started primary school when they turned six years old, and black children at seven years old.

I began my Grade one in 1975 at Chembira Primary School in Glen Norah (thanks to my sister Hlekiwe for remembering the name). In Grades three to five, I was sent to boarding school at

St. Mark's in Mhondoro along with my sisters Hlekiwe and Deliwe. Those two years (1977 and 1978) were the most formative years of my life. I learned to take care of myself physically and emotionally. I was at St. Mark's at the ages of 9 and 10 years old. Some of my classmates' ages at the time ranged from 9 years old to 20 years old- imagine!

This gigantic age difference between classmates was due to a multitude of reasons; some of which were economic, as some black families could not afford to send their children to school until they were teenagers. Furthermore, some school children did not have legitimate or accurate birth information. This meant that they were not able to register for school until they attained their birth certificates—this was very common during the colonial days.

My first week at boarding school, I was caught smoking. This was my very first attempt to smoke while hanging out with some older students. I had just taken my very first puff and I was coughing up a storm when the deputy Headmaster walked in.

I was literally caught red handed. There was a total of seven of us who were in this dormitory smoking. For our punishment, we were each lashed seven times. In addition to the lashing, we were suspended from school for two weeks. It was two weeks of gruelling manual labour repairing roads. I realized that my two-week suspension sentence had emotionally hardened me. As a result of that suspension, boarding school wasn't that bad.

We had to wash our own clothes. I had garnered respect from guys in higher grades because I never snitched or broke down. Furthermore, I earned a spot in the hierarchy of boys within the boarding school because I enjoyed fist fighting and I could hold my own. However, let me mention that after this incident I never smoked again or drank alcohol... up to this day!

I remember how one day an older boy (he was probably 14 or 15 years old) slapped my sister Deliwe. Even though I was younger than Deliwe, I was very protective of my sister. Deliwe came crying to me immediately after the incident and we both went after this bully. I was 9, and Deliwe was 11. We took care of him. Nobody ever messed around with me or my little-big sister Deliwe!

In 1980 Zimbabwe gained its independence. I remember how post-independence; most white families didn't want to live under a majority black-ruled Zimbabwe. Consequently, these white families started migrating to either white ruled apartheid South Africa, England, and Australia. As a result, houses in the predominantly white suburbs became available when those white families left Zimbabwe. Black families who had the resources began moving from the Townships to bigger and better homes in the suburbs.

We moved from Glen Nora to Lochinvar for a year and a half. Our family then moved to Mandara shortly after April 18th, 1980. This was a big deal for us because in the townships (like Glen-Norah where we grew up), our toilets were located outside the main house. This meant that we had no tubs and showers with hot water facets inside our houses. In fact, bathrooms in most townships had showers with cold water only. If one wanted the luxury of bathing in hot water, then one would have to physically boil the water using firewood!

However, when we moved to the burbs (or as we say in Zimbabwe: "kuma Dale Dale"), we suddenly had the same perks and privileges that used to be exclusive to white people. For instance, bathrooms were now inside the house along with showers, tubs, and heated geezers...mind-blowing!

Most homes in Mandara were fortified with concrete walls known as 'Durawalls'. Most homes had barking guard dogs and much to my shock, there were no neighbourly black homeowners in sight. So just like that, we were in a beautiful home. Even though the house was in an exciting new neighbourhood; the Lupafya family was isolated from chikwata (familiar groups).

Within a few days, my sister Deliwe (fourteen years old at the time) and my brother David (eight years old) brought home a friend each. They both befriended a sister/brother combo...Deliwe's friend was Yvette and David's friend was Heath. Yvette and Heath were white! These four musketeers (Deliwe, Yvette, David and Heath) were doing the unthinkable...they were the first people I ever knew to have friends of a different race. I watched from the sidelines in bewilderment as these four musketeers would go to each other's homes. Though the parents from either family didn't seem to outwardly protest, both sets of parents were venturing into unknown terrain at the time.

I was observing and analysing this fascinating unicorn at the age of twelve. Nevertheless, there were sprinkles of black families in Mandara in 1980. I befriended domestic workers' specifically gardeners and some of their children. They informed me that there were four black families in Mandara including ours.

I recall how as the first term holiday was winding down, my father and I were starting to feel the pressure of the second term starting in a few weeks. My brother David and I were going to attend Courtney Selous Primary School in Greendale. David would be starting in Grade 2, and I would be in Grade 6. My sister Deliwe was going to be in Form 2 at Oriel Girls High in Chisipite. Both David and Deliwe were good because they already had a friend each at their respective schools.

Back to my dad. Father was gifted with a two-page clothing and supplies requirement per child by Courtney Selous primary and Oriel Girls High schools. This was a whole different animal to what father was used to in the past, when my parents would buy school clothes and supplies as they saw fit. Now at the "Group-A Schools" as they were known that two-page list was a requirement, and not a request. As for me, my high level of stress was mostly from my lack of confidence in being able to speak English to the white teachers and school kids.

I remember how my first day at Courtney Selous School was such a surprise. My father dropped David and me at the school office, and I was surrounded by whites. The folks who worked in the administration office were all white. The headmaster was white.

They took David to his class, and I was led by one of the staff to my Grade 6 classroom. When I entered the classroom, I was in a state of hazy blur. I was ushered to a desk in the front. But before I sat down, I thought I had caught a glimpse of two black people. I told myself that it was wishful thinking. I think when I stumbled into class, they were in the middle of an English Literature lesson. Mrs. Caldwell had asked the class who wrote Oliver Twist. I'm 13 seconds into this class and I thought to myself:

"Everyone knows it's Charles Dickens", but I was too embarrassed to answer because it would have been too soon, and I didn't want to be that guy.

Half a minute went by, and some white kid answered 'Charles Dickens'. I turned around to connect the voice with the face and I heard Mrs. Caldwell say: "That's correct, well done Tafi".

Something didn't add up. This kid looked like me but sounded whiter than the whites! In fact, his accent was not your typical "Rhodie" accent, and he sounded more British. I also observed a black girl in the classroom. What amazing luck! Three black kids in this class. As soon as recess began, I sprinted to the black kid (who at the time was surrounded by a lot of white kids). I inched my way to him and said in our Shona vernacular language: "Ma vet akawanda muno Shaz. Pakamuka vince tino batsirana" (translation, "We are outnumbered by the whites,

Bro. If any of them start anything, we got each other"). With a blank stare, this guy, Tafi left the classroom with all his friends.

Then I looked straight at the front of the class and saw a black girl sitting by herself. I went over and said to her: "Blaz anoda mangezi uyu" (meaning this guy really likes white people). The black girl didn't respond either. I was stunned. I automatically expected some sort of solidarity between the blacks. Nevertheless, as I stood in front of this black girl, she eventually introduced herself as Sylvia. She was from Zambia and didn't speak Shona. She told me that the black guy was called Tafi Chihota.

Furthermore, she said she didn't think he could speak Shona and she thought his family had just moved to Zimbabwe from England. Fast-forward today, Tafirenyika Chihota is one of my dearest friends of over 40 years. He is the only reason how I became part of the Township Brethren.

Much love to my brother Tafi.

My brother Alex, who is ten years younger than me had a different experience assimilating into the Group-A schools. For starters, he started at Courtney Selous in Grade 1. He has known his friend's post-independence till today. He has black friends and white friends, and they grew up together. On the other hand, I do not have any relationship with any white kids from Courtney or from Churchill Boys where I attended High school.

During high school, I was selected to be a Rotary International Exchange student and was sent to do a one-year exchange at a high school in Northborough, Massachusetts just outside of Boston.

This exchange program was from January 1986 to January 1987. At the time, my family in Zimbabwe concurrently hosted an exchange student from Pennsylvania. My classmates in Northborough were going to graduate in June 1987, and they wanted me to join them in June for our High School Graduation. To achieve this my classmates started a fundraiser, which they called the 'Bring-Frank-Back-Fund'. I remember how when I arrived at Logan airport in Boston, there were people with banners and TV cameras waiting for me because word had spread that Algonquin Regional High School was bringing back their African exchange student for graduation!

Fast forward kuma two Thazas…I am happily married to Tendai who is also from Zimbabwe. We live just outside Boston. We both grew up in the Townships. I was on the cooler side of St. Peter's Kubatana by way of Glen Norah and Tendai by way of 'Fiyo' (Highfields). We do have many memories of when we were young kids…ku Cee Jay watching Bruce Lee movies or crashing random weddings to get free cream sodas, kwa Machipisa, ku Highfields Public Swimming Pool to name a few. If you remember Bengal Juice or when Pork Pies were robust…then you are an O.G!

Peace!

Figure 1 Salisbury (Harare) 1970s

Figure 2 Salisbury (Harare) 1970s

Chapter Three: "Saints"

By Tapera Knox Chitiyo

SAINTS

UDI - RHODESIA GOES IT ALONE

Governor- General Dismisses Rebel Government

Verwoerd Assassinated

War to Hot Up, Warns Minister

Nelson Mandela Imprisoned

I am Not a Saint says John Travolta

Itai Cent Cent, Vakomana

Woolworth's Summer Sale breaks records

Umvukela, Umvukela, Zimbabwe

Richard Nixon Resigns

Cool Crooners cause sensation in Bulawayo

George Shaya leads Dynamos to 3-0 win

Hanzi varikuroja vese ne mbudzi

Frelimo takes over in Mozambique

Agreement at Lancaster House

A hot, windless day. 9 November 1976 in teapot- shaped Rhodesia. Dozens of us are hunched over our desks in the Beit Hall at St George's College, Salisbury. We wait. The tension builds. The Chief Invigilator looks up at the large brown clock with the silver Roman numerals. 2.00pm." You may begin," he says.

The examination paper reads:

The Associated Examining Board

For the General Certificate of Education

November 1976 Ordinary Level

Three Hours

Candidates will be supplied with four- figure mathematical tables and graph paper.

Slide rules may be used.

Calculators may not be used.

I read on, eyes glazing. Pages and pages of numbers and squiggles and signs. $4ix+18+ [yx+9]$ $i=2x+7yi$.... Wtf? On page 3, the multiple-choice section states that "marks will be deducted for incorrect answers." I look around; everyone is head down, burrowing into their exam paper. It's now 2.15pm. I'm falling, not flying. Sweat runs down my cheek. Then I relax. The tension leaks out of my pores.

Because I know that I have no chance, none, of passing this exam. I can't answer a single question. All I know is my name.

I'm gonna get a "U". Numbers are my chains. But it's ok. Because I'm keeping a promise, I made to myself. I am going to fail. I want to fail. Need to fail. I want paybacks for all those years of hating the subject. 2+2 =3. Fuck maths.

We are originally from the Makoni chieftaincy in eastern Zimbabwe. Our family totem is Tembo - the zebra. My great - grandfather Kagoro was a hunter. His son Tapera- my grandfather- grew up kumusha in Chendambuya, about 50 miles from Rusape. When he was a young man, Tapera went to Old Umtali to work. When my father MacLeod Ernest was born in November 1932, Kagoro walked the 70 miles to Old Umtali Mission to see his grandson. In those days most transport for Africans was on foot, or "chikochkarti "[scotch cart] or, rarely, by bicycle. Great grandfather Kagoro walked. His journey brought joy and pain- delight at seeing his grandson; and pain when he collapsed and died a few days later, worn out by the journey. But even as they grieved for Kagoro, the family also believed that that his newest grandson- father- must be destined for great things, to honour Sekuru Kagoro's spirit.

Grandfather Tapera moved up in the world. He was good with his hands and smart with numbers and the missionaries liked him and he watched how the black men drove the buses made by the white men. He learned how to take an engine apart and how to put it back together. He became a driver and in due course he saved enough to buy a bus. He moved to Salisbury and married Catherine Dzikiti - my grandmother. We have a late 1940's sepia photograph of them. Grandfather, dressed in his finest suit, looks confidently at the camera. Next to him is Catherine. Her eyes are big and round and fearful. She has clearly never been photographed before. Grandfather holds her hand to reassure her; scared but resolute, she holds his hand for dear life. My sister Cathy, granddaughter of Mbuya Catherine, will, decades later, display that same determination.

Grandfather's business - Makoni Bus Service-took off. He lived with his family in Harare [Mbare] township at 67 Sanyanga Street. Grandfather grew rich. For a time, he owned a Rolls Royce, the first black person in Rhodesia to do so. White men came to see him and his huge, shiny car. Sometimes Grandfather would take his neighbours and friends for a drive in the black "Roro Roycee". He was celebrated. He also had a shop in the Stoddard Square. I remember going there when I was a kid and Grandfather giving me black and rainbow - coloured liquorice and sugared doughnuts to eat. Eventually grandfather would go bust, but he'd made his mark. Chitiyo Street in Mbare is named after him. I still remember him - very dapper - always dressed in a suit and tie, even when he was relaxing at home. And he usually wore a black Homburg hat. Remember? The one with a neat ridge down the middle. Sekuru Tapera had a soft voice that carried the promise of reward if you did things his way, and drama if you didn't.

Dad grew up with his brothers and sisters in Harare Township. He went to Chitsere primary school, then on to secondary school. Mom grew up in the east with her parents the Reverend Luke and Mrs. Esther Chieza; and her siblings, on Dora Estate about 30 miles out of Umtali. Rev Luke Chieza was a Methodist circuit preacher who taught the Word in churches and homes around Manicaland. Sekuru Chieza was a temperance man- he didn't drink liquor, but he loved tea with condensed milk. He was never wealthy but he and Mbuya Esther worked hard to raise their family. I used to love going to see them ku Dora. Mbuya would open her arms wide in welcome and shout, "Noki na Kety, vazukuru wangu- heh, heh, mauuuuya!" Her strong accent, Manicaland's finest, was so warm and beautiful, like coming home. Diko, true!

The two families were acquainted, and dad and mum knew each other from high school. They met again in South Africa. Dad was a medical student at Natal University and Mom was training to be a nurse at MacCord hospital in Durban. In January 1959, McLeod Ernest Chitiyo and Wynona Beulah Chieza were married in the Stoddard Hall in Harare Township. In the photographs they look radiant, poised, eager for their new life. Their wedding was described by the local press as the Wedding of the Year. Everyone was there. By 1960, they had both qualified as medical practitioners.

Me and my sister Cathrine arrived in the early 60's as our parents worked the frantic hours of their profession. We stayed for a few years at Port Herald, Malawi where dad was the District Medical Officer [DMO] there. We then lived briefly in Highfields Township before dad was posted to Ndanga hospital, 35 miles from Fort Victoria, as the DMO, with mom as Nurse in Charge. We lived in Ndanga Township, near the hospital. Our house always had visitors; friends, relatives, those in need; and sometimes a friend who'd gotten blind drunk and needed to sleep it off. There were other visitors too. I remember vividly pointing and laughing at two large green worms writhing on the grass a few feet from me. Then mom screaming and grabbing me and bundling me back into the house. Those green skins were not worms; they were newly hatched green mambas....

Mom and dad kept in touch with their peers. Their generation were the medical change makers who proved that blacks could be as good as or better than whites in any field. They included Steven Parirenyatwa, Silas Mundawarara, E Pswarayi, Alfred Mutasa, Sipho Zwana, Oliver and Muriel Munyaradzi, Stella Madzimbamuto, Mrs. Rogers Magore and many more- their stories yet untold. They were the original township boys and girls; and they were also a mid- century network for change in Rhodesia. We owe their generation a huge debt.

They were also determined to give their children a good education.

It's late afternoon January 1967. I'm standing at the entrance to St Michael's Preparatory School for Boys in Borrowdale, Salisbury. I cry as my parents' green Opel's taillights fade into the distance. They are making the long drive back to Ndanga. Next to me is a large black tin trunk containing my belongings. I'm confused. The building is full of white women in long grey and white dresses, and strange coverings on their heads. They are nuns- they show me to the dormitory where I will meet the others. These others are all white boys. They stare at me, not with aggression but with curiosity. An African? What's he doing here? One of them comes up to me, runs one finger along my left cheek, then does the same thing on the other side of my face. He looks at his hands as though expecting to see his fingers covered in black soot. But his hands are the same colour they've always been. He shows them to the other boys. They laugh.

The nuns at St Michael's [we called it "St Mick's or "St Mix"] were firm but fair. They included Headmistress Sister Enda, elderly and grey haired; and Sister Maria, who was young and tall and had long black hair; and old, frail Mrs.

O' Connor. She had a long thick battered wooden ruler held together by reams of sello-tape. Mrs. O Connor taught English -if you didn't pay attention, you'd get a whack from that ruler and then you'd pay attention. Most of the kids got along ok. During break-time, we'd play marbles in the sandpit; or run around the playing field, or just chat. There were very few black kids at St Michaels - only three of us in my grade year initially; me, Tererai Munyaradzi and Thabo Zwana. Our fathers were doctors and friends, so we became fast friends. All the years that I was at St Michaels, there were never more than twenty black kids there. Being kids, there were sometimes arguments and pushing and shoving and swearing. Occasionally it was racial.

"Hey you, picanniny. Africans are stupid!" Then of course, you'd have to reply "Whites are dumb! "Stuff like that. We all talked to each other, but we hung out with our own people. St Mick's didn't segregate us - the school was all about racial mixing, in defiance of government policy at that time. But we kid often segregated ourselves.

At St Mix, I once went from zero to hero to zero in fifteen minutes. I had a leaky, leathery old football which we pumped up just enough to play football during break-time. Everyone joined in and because it was my football, I was made captain. The first few minutes were fun - a melee of kicking, passing, and shoving past your opposite number. But the ball was gradually softening, and with it my popularity. Pretty soon the ball was flat again. The game ended abruptly, and with it, my sudden stardom. Amidst curses and jeers, I was sent back to nowhere land.

But some things weren't funny. One day, Donald Wildling, a family friend, came running; "Did you hear about your friend Tererai?"

"What about Tererai? Where is he?"

"He fell and got hurt really badly. They've taken him to the hospital".

"What? Maiwe zhangu!"

Terry had been playing on the Jungle Jim, a structure of vertical and horizontal steel ladders. Someone had dared him to walk along the top ladder, eight feet above the ground. He'd tried, then slipped and fell, smashing his face onto the steel rungs as he tumbled. It was horrible, and Terry suffered facial injuries. Fortunately, he didn't crack his skull, as the Jim was built on sand rather than concrete; but he bore permanent facial scars afterwards. We were all shaken, and it was nearly a month before he was able to come back to school, now wearing false teeth as a permanent reminder of his heroics.

I completed Standard Three in 1971 and wrote the entrance Exam for Hartmann House, the intermediate school between St Michael's Primary School and St George's Senior School. I nailed English and failed Math- the shape of things to come. A week later, the results came - the combined score was a failure. I had never imagined that I would fail this exam; that I could fail. I cried the whole day. Mom was grim faced [Dad was abroad, writing his examination to become the country's first black pathologist]. Then Mom said to me, "Don't give up; I'm going with Mrs. Munyaradzi to see Sister Enda." Tererayi had also failed- he had soared in math and plunged in English. So, our mothers went to see Sister Enda to plead our case. She in turn went to Hartmann House; she didn't ask them; she told them that we should be admitted; or else. Sister Enda had grown up in Ireland and lived through the Troubles there; when she put her mind to doing something, nobody said no. Tererai, and I were admitted to Hartmann House. We were in! I thank them all.

I was at Hartmann House "[HH]" in 1972 and 1973. I was extreme in two subjects - in Latin, I set a school record of 100/% in five successive Latin tests and followed up with 100/% in the Latin exam. To top that off, I won the 1973 HH Latin Prize. HH Headmaster Mr. Parsons handed me the Prize at the ceremony. "Well done," he said, giving me a firm handshake and a bigger smile. I felt good. Mr. Baldy having to hand me the Prize felt like payback for all my days of torture in his math class. But Parsons wasn't done with me just yet; the name engraved on my Prize was Tererai Chitiyo. Ndizvo! Terry doubled over with laughter. All us darkies look the same, right? Terry would tease me for a long time afterwards, saying that the Prize was his too. What could I say? He was right. I laughed aloud.

I was good at English too. But I set another record; 7% in the maths exam; rated "the worst ever!" by the maths teacher, tough, red-faced Mr. Parsons. He had a large round face, with long hair around the sides of his head. And a glistening bald patch in the middle. His nickname was "Mr. Baldy." He didn't like me. "Useless, bloody useless!" he'd mutter, in his deep Australian accent, throwing my homework book at my face. One day he brought a strange cone- like hat with a big red "D" marked on it; He walked to where I was sitting in class and pressed the cone onto my head. "Know what this is?" he thundered. I shook my head. He prodded my forehead with his meaty index finger. "It's a bloody dunce's cap; dunce means a thicko and that's what you are. A black thicko. Stupid. You're going to wear it from now on until your grades improve." My grades never did improve, so I wore the cap in every Maths class. And maths was every day, sometimes twice a day. "Stupid" - prod; "stupid" - prod; "bloody black fool, aren't you." Slapping my head hard each time he spoke to me in class. Slap. Jab. Jab. slap. His language, his rhyme, never mine. Five times a week. For two years. But I wasn't the only one; Mike

Mallaghan, a gifted singer- he got the dunce's cap too, for Latin and Maths.

HH was ok, but Rhodesia wasn't, and this filtered down more and more. Some of the white boys didn't want to come close. "My dad says we should stay away from kaffirs - they smell." We played on the same sports teams, but we weren't allowed to join the white kids in away games at the white schools. We learnt about Henry VIII and his six wives, and the Tudors and Stuarts in England and Scotland, but we also knew that in the breathed- in, breathed- out air of Rhodesia, that colour was everything.

Prime Minister Ian Smith was once a surprise guest at our 1973 HH morning Assembly. Everyone stood up when he came in - everyone except Tererai. He didn't stand up and because he was my best buddy, neither did I. I didn't stand up for Smith. It wasn't courage; it was just instinct. We couldn't stand up for him. We just could not. Even at age 12, we knew that Smithy was wrong, all wrong. So, there we sat - two black peas in a sea of white rice. The school saw it, and Ian Smith and Mr. Parsons, up there on the podium; they saw it. I thought Mr. Baldy was going to explode. Afterwards, we got twelve cuts each from Mr. Parsons and another twelve with the cricket bat from big Dave Bawden the sports Master. For two weeks afterwards it hurt to sit. But we'd made our little point. And we hadn't stood up when Smithy left either. They put all that in our school reports. Dad read my report.

"Saka, Mister" - he always called me Mister or Tapera when he meant business- "what's this?" He put the report on the kitchen table and looked again at me. Something in his face, in his eyes; a twinkle, like sunshine? "You didn't stand for Ian Smith. Good!" he said, and that was that.

I don't know what Tererai's dad said to him.

We say Sssss...

Say WHAT?

Say SAINTS

S.A.I.N.TS

Saints Saints Saints Saints!

[Saint George's College War Cry]

January 1974. I'm at St George's College Jesuit School, just off the Borrowdale Road. We, the Form Ones, are FNB's [F.....g New Boys]. We're outside Pre's Room [Prefects Room] and two luckless Form 2's are demonstrating the War Cry. They aren't shouting with enough enthusiasm, so they must do 50 press-ups each. Earlier, the FNB's had been welcomed by the Rector, chubby, bluff Father Henry Wardale. Then we're each given five typed pages of St George's History and the lists of all the Prefects and First X1 cricket and rugby and swimming and... Everything.

"You'll be tested on this soon" says Wardale, smiling grimly.

And we were tested for sure. Week three was officially Prefects week but we knew it as Hell Week. For that week, any senior was free to interrogate any Form One they saw. We crammed the information ahead of the days of thunder, but to no avail. "When was St George's founded?" "Do the war cry... louder you little shit!" "Is Godfrey Wright First Eleven or First Fifteen?" "You don't know? Are you fucken stupid?" "Yurra, why do they allow bloody kaffirs like you at this school? Fucken houties.... where's your spear?"

No one was spared, and if you messed up, they took you to Pre's room for a working over; head, hands, and feet. No use hiding in the toilets during break either; the seniors were wise to all the tricks- "all Form Ones out: we know you're in there!"

So long ago, and some things have faded from my theatre of memory. But here's old Father Tom Creaghan puffing away on his pipe in the school library, a wonderful sanctuary of books. It became my favourite room. I met many writers, the living, and the dead, in there. I had numerous conversations with their words. But it wasn't all highbrow. During the holidays, I loved to read comics, Superman and Batman and The Avengers. And also, South African comics, especially She. She was a caped black crime fighter with superpowers and The Knife of Life. She always fought and beat the bearded dastardly villain, The Vampire and his Glove of Death. She was good and kind and strong. And best of all, she was pretty and voluptuous, an ebony icon who wore her skimpy outfit with panache.

We loved that comic. She was township literature. And Rhodesia had its own black heroine; in 1973, local supermodel Kubi Chaza featured in the James Bond film Live and Let Die. That made waves, big ones, at all the bioscopes. Kubi instantly became every black dude's pin-up. John Indi, her future husband, also broke barriers when, in the role of Shakespeare's Othello at Reps theatre, he kissed his white leading lady, not once, but many times. In public. And she didn't mind one little bit. That got people's attention.

And now here are look- alike science teachers, Fathers Hugh, and Michael Ross. There's Father Brewer, a quiet Afrikaner chain smoker who taught Latin. And Father "Jock" Edwards, the tall English language and rugby teacher. And curly haired, florid George McKenna, who taught Chemistry. I was crap at Chem, so George and I weren't the best of friends. Once, when I asked him what the symbol in an equation meant, George replied, "It's a spear!"

And over there is ruddy- faced Pete Turner, the Englishman who had driven his battered Land Rover from England to Rhodesia in 1971.Turner was the PE teacher. He wasn't impressed when I finished waaay back in the inter- house cross - country: "I thought all Africans can run...!". But I was decent in the 100 and 200m sprints and was drafted into the under 13/15/15s rugby team. Now, here's geography teacher Baron "Grinner" McKenzie of Red castle. He dished out the ferrulas ["feds"] - hard slashes to the hands with a piece of whale bone. McKenzie seemed to get off on it- laughing with each whack- and dammit, those feds hurt, especially on a cold winter morning. Saints had no black teachers then - only workers who laboured in the kitchens or on the grounds or drove the tractors and the school bus. Sometimes they'd whisper "Pamberi ne macomrades." to us. "Pamberi", we'd reply. Old Mr. Sithole, the school driver, loved that call and response. His usually solemn face would crease in a wide grin.

There were some mixed-race teachers- young, brilliant, explosive Mr. Fernandes, the Maths Teacher, and chubby Mr. Ross Antao, the French teacher from Goa. And there was Mr. Gamaroff, also a French teacher; he looked like a hippy with his long hair, beard, and earrings. Oh, and there was Walter "Wally" Dewar, who ran the stationery department. Wally was a veteran of the First World War - his index finger was shot off at Ypres in 1915. He'd retrieved it somehow and kept it in a jar of pickled water. He'd show us his bottled finger with a flourish and a gleeful laugh. There was also quick talking, insightful Father Rea, who became my history mentor after an initial falling out which led to me being summoned by the Rector. There weren't many female teachers in my time, but I remember small, quiet Mrs. Trimming, who taught Science; and elderly Mrs. Crozier, whose husband also taught at Saints. And tall, young, pretty Miss Stafford, who got a lot of guys' pulses racing.

In 1974, Prefect Steve Bradbrook ran a record 10.8s for the 100 and won everything at the inter-schools too. We screamed a lot of war cries that year because the first team rugby was unbeaten until their last match. But some things stayed the same; me and Luckstone Mareya were coming from lunch, when a Form Six

Senior told us to stop. He walked up to us, stared at our faces, hawked up a wad of yellowish phlegm and leisurely spat on each of us in turn. The spit dripped down our faces. Passers-by looked away. The Prefect watched, then he laughed and walked off, whistling.

We got along ok with most of the white boys in our year, except when the K- word shuttered conversation. Tererai's father was abducted by the police in 1975 - bundled into a car in broad daylight at Harare hospital, where he was a surgeon. We all feared for his life, and his family wouldn't see him until Independence. Tererai became even more outspoken, and more than once, he and I stood shoulder to shoulder, fists primed, hitting, and getting hit, as the race boys fell on us. We were raw. Raw like amacimbi.

During the holidays I'd sometimes hang out in Highfields- around Mushandirapamwe Hotel or just walk around or meet up with local guys like fast-talking Mike Katsere or the Mataures or the Chingokas, who knew everyone. There were also a lot of pop festivals in those days- you could hear local guitar heroes like Manu or Louis Mhlanga, and bands like Dr Footswitch or the New Tutankhamen or Wells Fargo. Rufaro Stadium, Glamis Stadium, Saratoga nightclub, all hosted great live music. But the festivals were also a great place to try and chuff up the girls and there were always hot soul sistas to check out at the shows. Look, but don't touch. We were living in Marimba Park suburb then - all the families knew each other and many of us went to the same schools. The Kaharis, the Mundawararas, the Mushores, the Muhambis, the Kuwana's, the Mutiziras, the Shoniwas, the Magores and so many more. Marimba was next door to Mufakose Township, where we'd often go to play slug and bet, dollar, dollar, against the local shashas. Sunga ma net!

Itai Cent Cent vakomana

ini ndachona, ndibatsirewo

ndapota, ndashaya zvekuita

hurombo huroi

kanausinimari, hauna hushamwari

[Popular 1970's tune by the Tutankhamen Band]

Sekuru Tapera died in 1974.We buried him kumusha. In 1975 my cousin Godwin Ngosi and many of his classmates disappeared. No one knew whether they were dead or alive although there were whispers that they had joined the struggle. In 1976 the Rhodesians attacked Nyadzonya Camp in Mozambique killing hundreds of Zimbabweans. All the black guys at Saints were ashen faced when we heard about it. But I remember some of the white guys laughing and saying "You, see? That's what happens to fucken terrs. I hope they kill many more." A few weeks later I was on the front pages myself - actually, my first cousin and namesake Tapera Ernest Chitiyo, who was hanged at age 19 for being in "possession of weapons of war". We went to see him the day before he was hanged. He showed no fear and told us to be strong and that the country - Zimbabwe- would be liberated. For weeks afterwards the white farmer boys looked at me suspiciously. But I was big, too, and another boy in my year, Ken Matsikidze, had previously done us all a huge favour. Ken wasn't large, but he was solidly built and a tough Karanga from Masvingo. He and a farmer boy decided to sort each other out. Campbell, the white guy, was big and tall, a natural athlete. We feared that he would give Ken a beating. But it was Ken- smaller, faster, more compact- who hit with more accuracy. His right arm blurred, there was an urgh-hh! Suddenly there was a lump over the white guy's eye. He lashed out wildly, but Ken swayed back slightly, then came back from another angle. Faked a left then pushed a straight right to his opponent's face. Now Campbell was bleeding from the nose and his eye began to puff up. When he picked up something - a knife? -we all scattered. But Ken was a hero after that.

At home and even at school, we had friends of all races. We didn't waste time hating those who hated us. And many of the white guys in my year and above and below were cool most of the time. We could converse, not about politics, but about everything else. I remember once having an utterly weird and wonderful discussion about Jean Paul Sartre, Existentialism, Robespierre, and Chief Rekayi Tangwena, with my brilliant classmate Graeme Harrower, and our French A-level teacher Mr. Antao. But the war was biting- you'd come back to school after the holidays and hear that so and so had been shot and killed at his farm; or that so and so had been "killed in action". Guys like Simon Musto, Leroy Duberly, and Bruce McKend. Such a waste of life. The St George's school chapel had paintings and glass frescos of Christian saints and martyrs. Now it was hosting a lot of Old Georgian funerals.

More blacks were coming to the school and in 1977 we had the first black teacher Francis Mazhero, who taught Geography. Francis had the biggest, funkiest Afro since Michael Jackson, and he looked a lot like Sly Stone. He was a cool dude. He wasn't that much older than us, and was like an older brother. Some of the whites hated having to call him "sir"; we loved hearing them say it. Godfrey Dzvairo, who was two years ahead of us, and who we called "Comrade Godey", would always fill us in on what was happening in the war. He promised that he would join the "boys," but he was arrested before he could do so and was only released in 1980. We watched and listened to the Rhodesia Broadcasting Corporation for sports updates and surreptitiously tuned our pocket radios to the Voice of Zimbabwe and the Voice of Resistance for real war news.

There was a lot of tension between blacks and whites at school, but we mostly tried to get along. Apple-pied beds were always good for a laugh, and we had to take a team approach in many things. Meanwhile, the Indian and Coloured and Chinese guys at Saints had their own stuff going on. Bruce Lee's Enter the Dragon put a spring in the step of the Chinese guys at Saints - the Lee's, Kee's, Majoe's and Chee's. And maths whiz See Ying Tommee was the funnyman in our year; a guy once did a loud, ripping fart, and See Ying yelled, "Open your ass and smell the gas!"

That brought the house down. But the white boys didn't want to mess with the Chinese guys - except to call them all "Broooce!" There were some talented guys in my year- Head Boy Paul Roche was an all-rounder who captained the national schools cricket team. And big Peter Allum, son of the Rhodesia Police Commissioner, was a nice guy and a good swimmer. And there were surprises; Mike Partridge - the biggest, fastest, scariest guy, with fists like anvils when we were in Form One...well, Mike mellowed in subsequent years, became Deputy Head Boy, captained the First Fifteen rugby team, and won the Most Popular Award in Upper Sixth.

There was plenty of black talent too- James Mudeke was a science genius; and gravel-voiced Felix Ntutu from Bulawayo was a natural footballer who would go on to play for Zimbabwe. And lean, fast, Rodrigues "Roddez" Nazare, was a record breaker in cross- country and exams.

We did have fun - like at the school dances where it was always a contest to score with a girl. And that's where we black guys - we called ourselves the "Soul Train" - honed our smooth talking, pick-up lines.

We'd spend the days before the dance practicing dance moves. Sometimes it worked. I kissed a girl at the dance, a white girl, for a dare. I could tell that she felt something for me. She kissed me back; yeah! A real integrated smooch- but that's as far as we went. Forbidden fruit. This was Rhodesia after all; and we wanted to show black girls our love too.

I was starting to get into music. Dad was an amateur guitarist and we'd grown up with music in the house; and Mom's family the Chiezas were natural singers. So, I started to mess around with dad's guitar, listening to BB King, Hendrix, Santana and local Shona and Ndebele music. Tony Zwambila from Bulawayo was the musician at Saints.

Guitar, piano, bass, drums, Tony could play them all. I'd watch him and then listen to the records repeatedly. Saints had other talented musicians-The Khan brothers, Lacerda Pahla, Farai Mpedzisi And Manuel Bagorro, an other- worldly classical pianist. I practiced, and eventually they said I was the second-best guitarist in the school, after Tony Zwambz. Bagorro played piano on the hymns at morning Assembly. Occasionally Father Brewer asked me to play the Assembly hymns on guitar. That would make my day. Then I heard George Benson and realized that I didn't know shit about playing the guitar. That's when I got serious about playing. Tony had left by then and I'd inherited his title. I got a few guys together and we put on a music show in 1978.

We started listening to Bob Marley and Jimmy Cliff. Jimmy's film "The Harder They Fall" was a big hit among black audiences in Rhodesia. He also looked like a "mucomrade" in the war, so blacks really related to him. I also listened to disco, rock, and to a local hero from Mushandirapamwe called Thomas Mapfumo. Hokoyo! And a wild British group called the Sex Pistols and their song Anarchy in the UK. Everyone, black, white, and blue loved the song because it was so angry.

We put a Shona riff to it. I still listen to it sometimes when I'm in a punk mood.

There was one strange incident back then. I was in the school music room, playing "Let it be" on piano, when I sensed this very large presence. I looked up, and standing behind me was Leslie Dunlop, Campbell's brother. Leslie was a year younger, but even bigger than his brother- he was massive, and he hated blacks. I thought -oh shit...! In that confined space, no weapons to hand, no question that he would fuck me up if we fought. But Leslie just watched and listened.

Then, astonishingly, he asked, "can you show me how to play that?" So, I showed him C, G, D and A chords on that ancient piano with its black and white keys and left him to practice. It felt like a human moment. For ten minutes there was peace in that tiny corner of Rhodesia. But a week later, Leslie was complaining; "those fucken munts...."

1979 was the year the war really hit home; 7.62mm FN-AL and 7.62mm AK 47 bullets brought death enough for everyone. So many lives of all colours, cut short. Grievance and grief. The fog of war. The dead buried themselves. Opposite St Georges is KGV1 Barracks. Every day, we'd hear the flat crack of FN rifles and the loud da da da da of machine guns as the soldiers trained in how to kill more blacks. Often, we'd hear the chigwa gwa gwa of a helicopter passing overhead.

On TV they'd show piles of black bodies, intestines out, bullets in, outside some army or police station. The camera would pan to show a white soldier or policeman casually smoking a ciggie as he surveyed the day's kill. But sometimes you could see that the hand holding the cigarette was trembling. The tea pouring from the Rhodesian teapot was blood red.

The war continued and talk of a black call-up to fight the "terrs" worsened the mood. When Francis Zindoga, one of Prime Minister Abel Muzorewa's ministers, sent his son to study at Saints, the hard men nearly assaulted the youngster. "Where's your bloody AK?" He only lasted a term. We wrote our "A" levels as the Lancaster House talks dragged on. Peace seemed such a distant drum.

12 November 1976. We're in the Beit Hall at St George's. We are writing the AEB "O" Level English Language Exam. At 1.55 pm, the Chief Invigilator tells us that we can turn over the papers, but we cannot start writing. At 2.00 pm, she says that we can start. At 2.05 pm, I smile. This time, I'm flying, not falling. Words are my wings. I'm gonna get an "A". I just know it. I'm keeping a promise I made to myself.

Three years later, at the annual Form 6 School Leavers' Tea, Father O' Halloran, who in 1977 had succeeded Father Wardale as Rector, asks me.

"What will you remember most about Saints?"

Tough question. I think hard for a minute. Then I look at him and say -

"Everything."

Chapter Four: The Making of Canderton Infrastructure Group

By Derek Zhanje

Introduction: The Mbare boys

My name is Derek Zhanje, and my life's journey has been nothing short of a rollercoaster ride through the vibrant tapestry of Harare, Zimbabwe. I hail from a family of four, rooted in the heart of Harare. Our story begins in the cozy embrace of Beatrice Cottages, a quaint section nestled in the bustling suburb of Mbare. My educational odyssey commenced in 1974 at Chitsere Primary School, a government junior school echoing with the melodic tones of Shona. As I treaded the academic path, destiny led me to St Martins Primary School, a multiracial haven where diversity bloomed. This move marked the beginning of my exploration into the mosaic of cultures that coloured our world.

When I reached Grade 3, my parents made a life-changing decision for my brother and me. They believed early English education would open doors for us, so off we went to St Martins Primary School, a vibrant Catholic institution nestled not far from Mbare in the heart of the then middle-income suburb, St Martins.

Picture this: a school teeming with diversity, where every corner echoed with the voices of white, Indian, and coloured learners. Our teachers and administrative staff were predominantly

Caucasian, making St Martins Primary School a melting pot of cultures and ideas. Those years were a kaleidoscope of experiences, shaping my worldview in ways I could not fathom at the time.

After conquering primary school in 1980, my educational journey continued its adventurous course. I found myself at St John's High School in Emerald Hill, another Catholic school that embraced multiracial ideals. The hallways echoed with the dreams of young minds, fuelled by the promise of a brighter future.

Slaying Dragons at St. Georges College

But my story didn't end there. In 1983, I stepped into the hallowed halls of St. George's College, an elite institution located in the exclusive upmarket suburb of Alexander Park in Harare. Surrounded by lush greenery and the aura of privilege, I felt a sense of awe and excitement. Little did I know that this chapter of my life would be filled with challenges, friendships, and lessons that would shape the person I was destined to become.

These experiences became the threads weaving the tapestry of my life, forming the foundation of my dreams and ambitions.

This institution, with its rich history, was a melting pot of races and ethnicities. It stood tall in Alexander Park, an upmarket Harare suburb. Here, amidst predominantly Caucasian peers, I marvelled at the kaleidoscope of humanity that defined my days.

What fascinated me most about St George's College during that era was its intriguing blend of diversity and history. Imagine this: a multiracial school, predominantly Caucasian in its teaching staff and student body, which, remarkably, had been embracing other races since the late 1960s. This was a time when the government was pursuing a divisive policy of "separate development," yet here stood St George's, a beacon of inclusivity where excellence in academics and sporting endeavours were encouraged and celebrated without regard for racial background.

Even with significantly higher fees compared to government schools, this prestigious institution opened its doors to black children and due to the income barriers, it was academics, professionals, and business elites that took advantage of the opportunities. In those hallowed halls, where the spirit of equality triumphed over discrimination, students from different racial backgrounds came together. It was a testament to the school's commitment to education and excellence, making St George's College a renowned centre of academic excellence not just in Zimbabwe but across Africa. The very essence of the school embodied the idea that education should transcend boundaries, and that, to me, was truly inspiring.

Black Social Stratification.

As I grew up, I vividly recall how there was a social class structure in Mbare and then I learned to recognize it even in the other African suburbs my family used to frequent such as Highfields, Kambuzuma and even in Mufakose within which a section called Marimba was reserved for the well to do Africans. So, there was a group of relatively more affluent African people who stayed in Highfields called "KumaStones". The properties in this area of Highfield were larger and well-built such as those commonly found in the low density suburbs where relatively higher income white people lived, than the relatively low-cost homes characterising the rest of Highfields. Presumably the black African residents of kumaStones section were more affluent than the other folk that lived elsewhere in the suburb.

Life in Mbare was a tapestry woven with threads of social stratification. The palpable divisions between the haves and the have-nots were impossible to ignore. The dichotomy of wealth was starkly evident, from the affluent dwellers of "KumaStones" in Highfields to the migrants seeking prosperity in Beatrice Cottages. My parents, both respected professionals, offered us a comfortable life, yet the disparities surrounding us were a constant reminder of the challenges many faced.

In Mbare the more affluent black folk tended to migrate to "Beatrice cottages" a lower density section established as restricted accommodation for European prisoners of war during the second world war. My parents were middle income professionals; my father was a salesperson with a company car and my mother was a teacher.

In Mbare, the wealthier black families often found their way to "Beatrice Cottages," a neighbourhood with a lower population density. Interestingly, this area had historical roots as restricted accommodation for European prisoners of war during World War II. As for my family, we belonged to the middle-income bracket. My father worked as a salesperson, enjoying the perks of a company car, while my mother dedicated her days to teaching.

Growing up in my parents' home in Mbare, I had a comfortable life. But even within the boundaries of our relatively well-off neighbourhood, I was keenly aware of the struggles faced by children from less fortunate families in other parts of the suburb. While I could afford to go to school with money for milk and a bun or a drink, other kids could not. However, the government of the day used to provide supplementary nutrition "maheu" and milk which was covered by the school fees.

Politics Aint for the Timid!

I remember vividly the political atmosphere in our neighbourhood, teeming with politicians primarily associated with Zapu and Zanu political movements. Periodically, tensions would escalate between these rival factions with periodic heated confrontations, leading to raids on the homes of these politicians by law enforcement agents. It was a time of intense political fervour and often, skirmishes, etching memories of those turbulent days in my mind.

The fact that my parents were 'professionals" and respected members of the community, and further that they were also politically active, they always emphasized that we must aspire to do well in school to achieve economic emancipation and not embarrass them.

Amidst the political tempest that gripped our nation, my parents, pillars of the community, instilled in us the importance and power of sound education and self-improvement. The clashes between political factions were the backdrop to my formative years, highlighting the challenges of our time.

My recollections of life in the township, was that there was a distinct class system of upper, middle, and lower classes living within the townships and this system was a replica of the British system, and ironically this same system has been perpetuated after independence.

Politics Aint for The Timid for Sure!

Growing up, both before and during my time at St George's College, I witnessed the palpable tensions among African political factions. PF-ZANU and ZAPU were prominent players, and I couldn't help but feel that the white regime wasn't doing enough to mitigate these conflicts. Looking back, it seems this hands-off approach was an unspoken but deeply ingrained policy within the local government during that era.

I believe this chapter in our country's history stands as a grim testament to how mutual suspicions among rival political factions hindered collaboration against their shared adversary: the white Rhodesians. The deliberate efforts of the white Rhodesians to stoke division and rivalry between these factions, coupled with a lack of commitment to upholding law and order, cast a shadow over the nation. It was undeniably a sombre and regrettable period in our history.

The End of the School Days Is Not the End of Learning

After completing high school in 1986, I was confronted by a significant setback when I couldn't secure a spot in the Accounts faculty at university. Instead, I decided to enter the workforce. My first job opportunity arose at the Standards Association of Zimbabwe, where I learned the crucial importance of safeguarding consumers against substandard products. Shortly after, in 1988, I ventured into the financial services sector by joining Barclays Bank.

Banking on Barclays.

Working at Barclays Bank introduced me to a subtler form of racial discrimination. Despite a workforce comprising individuals from diverse racial backgrounds, disparities in career development tracks were evident. Certain roles and departments had fewer black employees. One such department was the bank's treasury division, where I was placed. Here, most staff, especially in management positions, were exclusively white.

Despite these challenges, Barclays Bank was making strides in promoting black advancement. During that period, they brought in Mr. Isaac Takawira, a former senior civil servant, who eventually rose to become the Group CEO of Barclays Africa. Mr. Takawira became a cherished mentor and counsellor, guiding me through my professional journey. His presence marked a pivotal moment, showing me the importance of breaking racial barriers and fostering a supportive community within the workplace.

Elephants can dance - the reorganization of an industrial behemoth.

After a brief stint in the Treasury Department at Barclays Bank, a new opportunity arose within the Group Finance division of the Anglo-American Group. Accepting the position placed me in a uniquely strategic role, enabling me to closely witness the evolution of the company's operations in Zimbabwe. This role also provided me with insight into the organization's thoughtful response to the shifting political landscape and economic changes. At its peak, the Anglo-American Corporation in Zimbabwe was a vast conglomerate, boasting an impressive staff complement of nearly 900,000 employees on its payroll.

During that period, the Anglo-American Corporation, under the bold leadership of seasoned businessman Roy Pascoe Lander, embarked on a significant transformation. Recognizing the changing global landscape, the management made a strategic decision to shift their focus to resources. Consequently, the corporation initiated a process of divesting from what they deemed non-core businesses, redirecting their investments toward resource-oriented sectors.

At that juncture, Anglo American Corporation had spread its investments across a diverse array of industries. These included ventures in banking with First Merchant Bank, financial services through Von Seidels Financial Services Group, mining operations like Bindura Nickel Corporation, and chrome production with Zimbabwe Alloys. They were also involved in forestry with Border Timbers, sugar production at Hippo Valley

Estates, agriculture at Glenara Estates, and even brick and pottery manufacturing at Willsgrove Brick and Pottery. Their portfolio extended to everyday items such as bread with Lobels and agricultural endeavours like growing oranges and flowers at Mazoe Citrus Estates. The corporation's expansive involvement mirrored a dynamic era of diversified business interests.

In my observation the management of Anglo-American Corporation was uncommonly progressive in that as they divested from non-core businesses they proactively sought to empower previously disadvantages blacks.

A Tragic Failure of Leadership - Nelson Mandela.

However, by the mid to late nineties things began to change in the country.

A significant development was an announcement by President Mugabe that triggered an adverse economic incident that came to be known as black Friday, when the currency, and the economy crashed unexpectedly in one day's trading session. But what we should all have accepted was that it was inevitable. I recall the President announced that "we have pressure from the ex-combatants. We need to acknowledge their contribution to the liberation of our country. So, we are going to give war veterans $50,000 once off pension payouts".

It was never clear where that $50,000 payout would came from…and the country's budget was already in significant deficit - The Minister of Finance frequently prefacing his presentations with reminders that the people of Zimbabwe need to brace for difficulties from the necessary austerity measures and "tighten their belts", but in the banking and financial services community we understood immediately what this humungous and unfunded burden on the fiscus meant for currency stability. That was when the country's slide into economic turmoil accelerated.

The President in office at that time rejected the counsel of professionals like his finance minister, the late Mr. Bernard Chidzero who had returned home to serve his country after being employed as an executive at the World Bank. It was unfortunate tragedy and as Nelson Mandela put it - the events unfolding in Zimbabwe reflect a tragic failure of Leadership.

I feel as if that was truly a season of bloodletting and corporate madness, where we Zimbabweans made a series of poorly considered politically expedient decisions that only served the narrow interest of the elite seeking short term advantage but created long-standing hardship for the generality of the populace.

No Price Is Too High

In my view that was the season when, essentially, we started to sacrifice our moral compass and values thus accelerating the ensuing associated social degradation.

Do not get me wrong, I do believe that President Mugabe was a good and visionary leader in many respects but, it is acknowledged that political expedience and unwillingness to relinquish political power was his albatross.

Land Reform

By the time the year 2000 came round, we started to experience effects of another poorly considered government policy aimed at realising economic empowerment called "land-reform". At that time, I was still with Anglo-American Corporation which owned extensive tracts of land across the country perhaps topping as much as twenty percent of the country's landmass. I recall how we in Group Finance Division spent a considerable amount of time unpacking this policy in trying to understand the ramifications and the responsibility of the corporate Anglo-American Corporation in addressing historical social inequalities and promoting redistribution of collective wealth and opportunity. Anglo American Corporation is notable in pioneering voluntary land redistribution to local communities at numerous locations across the country.

However, it turned out that the process of implementing the Government's land reform policy was neither transparent, democratic, nor straight forward. International funders, including the United Kingdom and the European Union, who had previously pledged considerable financial support to the program withheld the promised support in protest. Many people applied for land, including myself and many of my peers but nothing materialized.

Suspicions Abound

One thing I remember in the nineteen nineties was the palpable tension between black and white people.

There was tension that was building up progressively, and we began to see a heightened level of suspicion from white people, especially in the light of the political rhetoric of Black Empowerment and Land Reform. For that reason, white people were increasingly suspicious of ambitious black people, and yet prior to that period these same white people had been promoting black advancement, and even encouraging ambition.

The Initial Cost of Land Reform

But after Land Reform pronouncements I recall numerous previously successful companies facing financial difficulties and shutting down. Literally whole industries that had been vibrant along with careers sustained by the activities were destroyed as well as family incomes being dissipated. I associate these unfortunate events with the mindset of those afflicted by the post-traumatic syndrome that our liberators brought home from the liberation war and transmitted the psychological brokenness into poorly considered and thus ineffective policies which in turn contributed to the country's inevitable and widely reported economic meltdown.

I should mention that the socialist years of the nineteen eighties were a big contributor to the chaos that subsequently engulfed the economy. In the eighties, even whilst the country promoted and pursued polices of free education, free health, and other things the government was mindful of the need to promote a degree of free enterprise and facilitate the flow of much needed foreign investment capital. But by the time the nineteen-nineties arrived the politically motivated policies had effectively driven the country's fiscus firmly into deficit and prescriptions of international lenders where not implemented consistently. The result was that the economy's contraction accelerated, and our leaders confronted by frustrated and restless populace were looking for something they could give their supporters to show the gains of independence.... and that's how the land issue developed in the chaotic manner it did, and that became the last straw for our economy.

Goodbye Anglo Man welcome the Telco Guy

After my stint with Anglo-American Corporation, I sought exposure in the services industry and moved to Econet Wireless, an emerging telecommunications services operator, where I successfully leveraged my previous corporate experience and thereafter I transitioned into consultancy and entrepreneurship and I became part of the generation that was also developing and creating models of operating business that could be scaled and durable systems are built.

I feel like I have acquired a lot of transferable experience in that regard, and I have applied myself to building up our family business called Canderton which we launched in 2011. How it came about is that I always had a side gig while I was in investment management.

I was drawn to opportunities in infrastructure and real estate. My strategy for value accretion entailed "flipping" buying underpriced neglected apartments, bachelor pads, fixer uppers and focussing on fixing the kitchen, and the bathrooms and thereafter reoffering the property to market and then make a margin of profit.

As the surplus from flipping property grew, I was able to indulge my other interest in motor vehicles and got involved in car dealership trolling auctions and corporate defleeting - buying and selling second hand cars.

So, during my time engaging in these vocations, I generated significant supplementary income that enabled my family to move from the apartments to the suburbs and I transitioned from the Harare suburbs of Mabelreign, Strathaven, Avondale and then eventually we acquired property in Borrowdale Brooke. My family launched a retail business managed by my wife. Over the passage of time, I realised that balancing my schedule working full time and assisting my wife in operating my family business whilst engaging in other side ventures became too hectic.

Becoming a Community Man

Also, I was getting invitations to join boards outside of my employment. I was appointed a Director of BancABC a listed Financial Services Group with operations in southern and eastern Africa and held that office for 7 years of which for the later 5 years I was Chairman of the BancABC Asset Management business.

I joined the board of a Regional IT services provider distributing banking systems. I was also elected to the Board of the Zimbabwe Association of Pension Funds and in my second term of office was elected Chairman of the Investments Committee of the association.

This organ is the primary liaison of the Zimbabwe Pension funds with the Regulator and the Ministry of Finance and is demanding of time. I also accepted appointments to our Church board and oversight of church support services. I joined the boards and executive committees of the advocacy organisations Borrowdale Residents and Ratepayers association as well as the Wetlands Trust.

Against this background I was increasingly struggling to keep up with schedule and growing in my conviction to increase control over my life and my circumstances. I realized that the income now from our business was competing with the income from my formal employment and of course my peers. You know when money is flowing, it's visible, and I could see the resentment because even my boss, when he came to visit my house asked me "How did you get this place?" So, I could sense their discomfort and resentments and decided to commit to our business full time.

The first break in real estate investing.

Let me tell you how I started investing in real estate.

When I joined Barclays Bank one day this old lady - a talkative pensioner I would serve periodically, she came in saying "I don't know what to do; I want to go to Australia to be with my kids. I have been trying to sell my apartment and was now considering having it auctioned but you know they don't give you anything." So out of curiosity I said OKAY "How much would you want for your apartment?" she said "$18,000" which I knew i could not afford. I offered $12000 of which my savings amounted to $2000 which I explained to her that it was all that I would be able to release on signature of the agreement of sale with the balance coming from mortgage, and fortunately, surprisingly she liked me enough and agreed! In due course she gave me the apartment for that amount together with all her household contents and appliances furnishings - stove, furniture, beds, and the works! Literally walked into a ready-made home.

That's life! I hope anyone reading this will be encouraged and appreciate the importance of being nice to people because you never know where your break will come from!

Canderton Group is Born.

That's basically how I started my property development company and I've been operating ever since! Since I married my wife, she has been instrumental in shaping the vision and identifying emerging opportunities that have enabled significant growth. Lately we have managed significant scale developments including a shopping mall, development of a whole school campus, several churches, and numerous low income stands and houses and high-income homes.

Chapter 5: Seke
By Munyukwi Milton Kahari

Introduction

My full name is Munyukwi Milton Kahari Zinhumwe Chauruka Kunaka Zengeza Seke, and answer to any one of these names depending on where I am, I am Seke, and come from Mutangadura Village, Seke Materera and when among my fellow communal folks, Chakanyuka a variant of Munyukwi when my uncles are calling me, for the name Munyukwi is put in use when describing me in my absence (e.g. Who done this? Munyukwi did this) and Chakanyuka is the variant used when calling to draw my attention (e.g., Chakanyuka come over here). However, Milton in more popular among the younger and close maternal family members with older generation of Aunts more likely to call me Millie and the male counterparts Mhofu, or Seke and cousins call me Milaz.

Among the Seke royal houses they call me either Sonono or Kunaka when I meet those from the Motsi branch of family and Chauruka for those who are from the Sonono Kunaka branch, this obviate the need to remember my first name or my surname. It is only in the official spaces that my first name is used Munyukwi, this includes places of work, until I moved to Papua New Guinea where Milton has been my preferred name for obvious reasons.

I was born on the 9th of March 1966 at number 58 Crowbrough Way Mufakose, Salisbury, a house birth which was delivered by my uncle's (Absolom Ndoro) wife a nurse, Margret (nee Mutambanengwe) Ndoro. I am born to Elisha Tawonezvi (later Zacharia) Kahari, from the Royal House of Chauruka, Kunaka (Sonono) family of Seke (my father had chosen to use the nickname of his grandfather Ka'hari-meaning inside- which his grandfather had become the name he was known, as his surname, because he felt there were too many people using the name Seke) and Ellen Chitandara Ndoro a daughter of BSA policeman, Michael Chambiyango Ndoro, Detective Inspector Sergeant "concrete" for his tough attitude towards crime.

It is said that my paternal grandfather and namesake Munyukwi Zacharia Chinyamakanga Zinhurimwe Seke had to come down from Seke Communal Lands, just outside Salisbury, where he was acting Chief Seke after his young uncle Mtangadura who was Chief place of his late father had also passed away. The purpose was to authenticate me as of Seke genealogy. He named me after himself, Munyukwi because like him I had been born a boy of exact genealogy without intervention from the elders who would have required my parents to subsist on strict diet with herbs to increase their odds of male child. My father named me Milton after the Prime Minister of Uganda at that time Obote, because he said I was as dark skinned as Milton Obote. I was second child after my sister Angeline Fungayi Kahari, who in times went by her married name Mazaiwana after marrying George and later in her second marriage by name

Rowlette, after marrying Keith and lives in the USA. Eventually I will be the only boy in the family with six siblings.

I have been married since 1990 to Lynda Rosie Maisiri, we met at the Harare Polytechnic where the Bachelor of Technology programme was born and we have four daughters and yes, like my father did not entertain the herbs, I do not believe in science that is not explainable from first principles. At the time of writing, I was we were living in Papua New Guinea as expatriates, having moved over here in 2017 from Johannesburg, South Africa where we had spent the last 19 years.

Mutare – The formative Years

I first came to know I exist as something when I was 5 yrs., and I suspect from a hiding from my mother for one naughty behaviour or another, it was like waking up where you did not exist. My suspicion now as an adult is that I may have been partially deaf from fluid in my eardrums and therefore unable to receive instructions, which was correctly perceived by adults of that time that "haanzwe" (does not listen) and "musikanzwa" label. At some point a slap or something must have popped the ear and the fluids came out of my ears, it seems my coming to being, knowing I am somebody was instant. This was in the city of Umtali, where my father had been posted as a civil servant in the ministry of agriculture, cooperative department.

I was enrolled at a creche on a hill and aptly called "Church Gomo" about the age of 4 or 5 years and I hardly remember what is was all about until one day suddenly when I woke to my senses found myself to be the most feared creche member and no milk will start being distributed before I get mine and all the girls, cause I had sisters and was biased toward the girl child. We were neighbours with Judy Chinyanda family, Thomas Makore, and the late Churchill Kabefu. Churchill and I were brought up close, however he was a quiet obedient only child, whereas I was beating up everyone who dared me up and down the street. Parents would come home to complain that I had beat their much older children and would get emotional and attempt to beat me, my Mother, would punch them sometimes so hard they would fall on their backs, and will shout at them that they were primitive and she was the daughter of a sergeant and Shumba Nyamuziva (a lioness). So, yes mom and son were feared, later my father confessed that is why he decided to live away from townships.

I lived in Sakubva at a house with a big tree and occasionally some black man with a pellet gun would come to shot little birds and will give me the ones which did not die but got injured to nurse back to health, most of them died, maybe from infection or loneliness I can't tell, but I think it was infection with hindsight.

Umtali a border town was a hive of political descent, and I learnt politics before I could crawl, the reason being its proximity to Mozambique which was waging a bush war against the Portuguese. By 1971-2 as kids, we could hear loud explosion from across the border in Mozambique to the cheer of many. I remember riots of our fathers in the streets of Sakubva and the response of the authorities to those riots with dogs and teargas which filled the streets and my father, and his neighborhood friend come streaming in the house looking for a hiding place and my mother stuffing them in the wardrobe and behind them the police barging in pursuit. My mother, a tough woman standing in between the bedroom doors and front door and boosting of her credentials as daughter of a retired sergeant and the police backing away.

Highlights was going creche and going the bioscope occasionally with my uncles who lived with us whilst attending secondary school in Umtali. Occasionally we would host my mother's younger sisters too, Hosanna and Dorcas Ndoro for long periods of time. I later learnt from them in my adulthood that they used to visit during school holidays.

That was my first stint in Umtali, whilst we lived in Umtali every holiday I was shipped off to my maternal grandparents who had been allocated a farm in the Zviyambe African Purchase area. In the 1970s this was virgin land, and we could go hunting with the farm worker and return with exotic bush meat to give our grandmother.

At this farm during the holidays, I would rendezvous with my cousin coming from Salisbury, Highfield, Shongwe, a name my grandfather told us meant balanced rocks, he had given him this name, he was also named after my grandfather Michael a Christian name fostered upon. I spoke the Umtali dialect of the Shona language (Chimanyika) and he sought to mock me over it, which always ended ndichimunera (beating him up), in Umtali we spent most of our times battling in the streets or in the play parks in games of fighting called game giyaz (fighting with our feet), and we horned our combat skills, I did not know what they did in Highfields Salisbury, because Shongwe could not fight.

From the onset, my maternal grandfather would particularly target me for oral history and this man had the most influence on my values, he had sought to groom me so I could become the first Black police commissioner, he was an educated man with impeccable command of the English language and at times referring to himself as "British". The history was based on his own life journey on what he observed himself and later as I was a young man, he talked about history passed down to him until his death aged 95 officially but was much older cause he could not tell exact year he was born, but guessed his age as he joined the BSA Police Services. I later got to understand that this had been an undertaking he promised my paternal grandfather who died in 1972. In Umtali I made lifelong friendships from creche which were later re-enforced on my second stint in that City. My best friend was Marcos Makoni, later infamous at UZ in 1986, but there were others Tonderayi Sachikonye and his twin sister Sarah, we later in life we would meet at UZ in 1986.

Nyazura

By 1972 my father had been transferred to Nyazura a small sleepy rail town, serving the farmers between Umtali and Rusape, it had a new location (sub-burb) built and the house were new, street new as well as a new school and even much closer to Zviyambe and now I could see my grandparents more regularly.

One Christmas, my father drove us in his Austin Cambridge to Seke communal lands, my father had always had a car, he told me that he had a car first before looking for a wife. We arrived in the middle of the night after several fan belts breaking and my mother having to take off her lady stockings and these were retrofitted into a workaround fan belt and we proceed at snail pace until we get into Marondera and shops are closed, but ever helpful the people they run around in the night looking for "rinopindirana" (interchangeable with other models) fan belt. We still arrive at midnight and the whole village which was pitch black wakes up to great us enthusiastically.

My Aunt comes and greats me calling me baba vangu kani (my father) and we quickly are spread around to go sleep with cousins. I lose sense of time, how many days we are there, but I get into the thickness of things playing with other children and then demanding an old family heirloom which my grandfather kept Seke Knobkerry. When we were taking off, the villagers had persuaded him to give it to me and have kept this heirloom since. Soon after that visit we had to make a return trip the man who was over 98 yrs. or more had passed away, he had my father when he was in his late 60s in his third marriage.

Rusape Part I

After the funeral we moved from Nyazura to Rusape, we moved to Vengere Township, this township was to mould me into a tough nut to crack and build my confidence beyond my age.

I Started school at Vengere Primary school in 1973, and soon quickly integrate into the culture of the town, learning a queer lingo called Chibhende (folded language) in which you add Ps after every syllable, such as if you wanted to say "iwe" (you in Shona) you extended it to "ipiwepe". In this township I will meet Mozambique refugee children from the refugee camps right next to the township. Many kids were discouraged from mingling with them, but not me. Their stunted growth deceived you to think they were the same age as yourself, I became friends with one Frank Pindepinde, Franks family had graduated from the camps into the location. Later in life I would meet Frank at a Rhodesian check point in Auxiliary forces uniform, and in charge of search party, he promised to give a job once I turned 16yrs under his command, I was only 13 years old.

We spent most our play time learning to box preparing to fight on Sundays in the refugee camp before going to watch soccer in Vengere Stadium or swimming. The refugee kids because they were much older than us hit hard, unbeknown to us they were normally two to three years older than us. Some of the time we spent being extra naughty creating a reputation in the small township, we stole peaches from one chap who was reputed to have won the Rhodesian lottery and bought himself a jaguar, and we used to call him master skidder, for the stunts he used to pull when he noticed us lined up along the street and clapping hands shouting "master skidder, master skidder".

Across from the township over a swamp going close to the rail-line was probably the only mass seasonal employment fruit and jam factory, at the sound of the siren, women and men ran across the swamp to make it before the sound of the second siren. In this swamp with long grass and reeds, taller than a human we liked to think of ourselves as pirates and we had cut tiny paths to our hide outs. It was swampy for sure with dirty black muddy water. These swamps were ours, unless we were challenged by determined young couples who also used these swamps as rendezvous for exchanging affection, they were ours. We did not care much for the workers who took short-cuts through the swamps, in time we began to lay traps, such as tying together the grass from opposite sides foot path and disguise it, when they came streaming down that path running to catch the second siren, they would trip and fall over each other and we would shout " we have caught mice without hair" (Tabata mbeva isina vhere).

I remember one time a Muslim neighbour whom people in the township hardly socialized with passed away, and his compatriots came to mourn him. We were not familiar with Muslim culture, and it seemed odd to us as kids that a man would put on a long dress, longer than what our mothers put on and always white. We were afraid of this representation as much as we were curious. When they started their chants going around the house of the deceased we stood there perplexed by the ritual, however from the chants we made out what we thought they were chanting to be "Mahomed had farted on the tractor and holed it" (Mahomed asulila tirakita yaboka), so immediately as kids we start singing in a circle mimicking the mourners. This incident remained with me, and curious about Islam and have since made many friends of Islamic faith, I remaining nonbeliever.

Fast forward we were to return to Umtali, and I was in grade 3, at Vengere primary I had met interesting characters who I would meet later in my life at high school, Prince Makaya (Cranborne Boys High), Sam Buwu (Oriel Boys High) and Cyprian Marowa (University of Zim)

Umtali Second Stint

In Umtali we moved to an adjacent township from Sakubva, New Dangare and I was enrolled grade 3 at New Dangare primarily school and "pfacha" (suddenly) I meet Tonderayi Sachikonye and his twin sister Sarah who lived across the road from the school. Tonderayi immediately ran around the school telling everyone that the champion is back, and within hours I unexpectedly receive a challenge from a fellow in another class of grade 5. I refuse this challenge because I was extremely scared, did not know these people and attributed to them better capabilities than myself, given my experience in that town, which has been a lifelong problem (overestimating capabilities of others -Dunning Kruger Effect). They would not relent, discovering I had a little sister in grade 1, they went and intimidated her, and if there was something I could never stand for, is anyone bullying my sister of a girl. Although I had avoided altercation, as we left the school and I am consoling my little sister, who expected me to do something about it, trying to buy her a fat-cook from the ladies who came with hot fat-cooks after school. The boy accosted me and built little sand mounts in the sand in pairs depicting the breast of my mother and tries to kick the set of mounts as a sign of absolute disrespect, at that instant I launched a fist straight into his face. As he tried to retaliate, a flurry of fists caught him off guard and he was bleeding profusely through his nostrils.

Unbeknown to me this grade 5 pupil bullied all grade six and below, and I was in grade 3 going to 4 and by extension I was crowned the new bully from grade 6 below. Every school had to have an acknowledged bully we dictated what goes on and stopped class bullies from bullying their classmates without permission.

Buhera

We soon moved to Buhera district office, I was finishing my grade 4, to a little suburb built in a circle surrounding the District Administrator's offices. We were the only Black Family in that line and allocated a two bedroom of what used to be a guest house. I was enrolled for the first time into a rural school, Chikuvire Primary 4 km away and my sister Rumbidzai then grade 2 and I walked everyday with other black kids to that school. The daily walk was eventful, filled with stories, new friendships and sometimes fights, yes fights were never too far from me. At this school my teacher in grade 4 declared me a mathematics genius. I think this is for the first time I viewed myself in an academic way. Not long we were there, the empty bigger house that I always used to envy why we were not staying there was occupied by Rhodesian soldiers, they pitched tents all around the yard. There was a guava tree in that yard, so happens it had fruited, so I would go to the fence to get offered the fruits by the soldiers, but I did not understand a word of English they spoke. However, their presence indicated that war was near, my mother had not come with from Mtali, she had proceeded to Seke to build a modern house which was to be our sanctuary away from the war.

Seke - Homeland

We were shipped to Seke Communal Lands halfway through grade 4 to join our mother, my elder sister had since been sent to boarding school, Waddilove. We were enrolled Seke School, ironically built on the land on which originally my grandfather had built his home after they were evicted from the Goromonzi Ruwa area. He had given up the land under his uncle's insistence that he builds next to him, lest he not accept the chieftainship as he did not have enough people to defend it from his cousins' machinations.

My reputation as a scholar had to be defended, at Seke school I remained a so studious, but on the streets and herding cattle I packed a heavy punch, before long I was known to beat every boy two years older and below as far as my younger cousin Mushure Ronald Kahari would care to say how far, and he would go out of his way to seek fights so he could say Mukoma vangu (my big brother) will beat you up . I was happy here, I received respect from my aunts, who called me father and gave me local brew, and if anyone complained they would get a tongue lashing. They believed I carried my ancestors' fighting capabilities in particular Zengeza, who was a known warrior and fought alongside Mwendamberi (Gwenzi – his young uncle) and Mutasa (muzukuru).

I was to make connections with my extended family, many of them had never seem me, one cousin, Chamunorwa Ambrose Kahari a year older than me, was shipped from Bulawayo together with sister Ruth and their mom so they could be with us, lived close to the school and we spent time with them.

Rusape Part II

We only stayed in Seke for the remainder of the year, and we moved back to Rusape in 1976. This time we did not move to the township but found ourselves living in the foothills of Tandi overlooking the Rusape damn "KwaChindukuro" on a row of 6 houses with gravity irrigation and workers quarters, this settlement was for the land development officer (LDO), and it was so called, "kuma LDO", essentially small holder plots. These were government houses abandoned by the white officials who feared being killed by "terrorists" and were handed over to black officers in the related ministries. I was enrolled at a school which was across the river from Vengere Township called St Joseph's Primary School for my Grade 5.

The large plots had fruit orchards and fallow land for market gardening, however being some distance from the city where my father worked meant traveling costs were high for him and he needed to supplement his income, which he did by exploiting the installed infrastructure, market gardening. He was always short of labour and for what he was short off the children filled in the gap. I particularly remember extremely cold mornings picking green peas so he could take with into town to sell fresh.

What I most remember about this period was that my maternal grandparents would come frequently to visit mainly because my grandmother was ailing. She passed away sometime during this period. A little while after her passing and burial in Zviyambe, Pazororo Farm, my grandfather was to arrive hurriedly from the farm after surviving a lynching by jealous neighbours who has instigate the Zanu Pf fighters to kill him, on account of his service in the BSA Police service. He narrated a harrowing story, in which he was saved by his knowledge of history and was banished and spared the noose. Living with him meant I benefited from the oral history for many years to come.

Christmas holiday of 1977, I went to Salisbury to spent it with my cousin Shongwe, they had moved from Jabavu Drive, Highfield into 33 Guildford Crescent, Sotherton. We spent much of that holiday getting acquainted with yoghurt and hailing a taxi to drive us down to the shops, buy yoghurt and back home. Many families had returned from exile and made home in Sotherton, these included my cousins Richard Wakatama, Mischek and Peter Ndoro and they had brought with them a first world culture which I was completely blown by. The played tennis on the tarred streets of the suburb and spoke impeccable English which my anglophile father would have been proud.

Waddilove-School of Hard Knocks

I was not to return to Rusape, was shipped to join my sister Angie, cousins Shongwe and Tendayi Ndoro at Waddilove in Marondera farming district. Waddilove had a strong family history, my maternal grandfather once enrolled there for seminary studies before pulling out, my father and my uncle had been schooled here, and first met here, and later when my father was working in the district of the new farms Zviyambe did he meet my mom in a chance orchestrated by my uncle. From 1978 to 79 I would attend this school, learn, and pick many vices that I never thought I would pick up at that age or ever.

Met many people here, notable is Patrick Chirume, Lishon Karume, Allan Choruma, Moses Hwande (I later employed him as a factory worker in early 90s), Cassium Zindoga and many others who passed through this institution. We were to coalesce as newcomers and others to avoid being bullied into a gang we later named "Danger Perigo" a name I was reminded a few years ago by Lishon, an odd name for a gang as Perigo is Portuguese for danger. After 1979, my mother had moved to Salisbury, into the suburbs in Park Meadowlands, change was coming.

The Encounter-War

One evening after escaping from the dormitory after the prescribed lights off and sleep time as usual into the edge of the bushes. This was a usual event for the gang, as we adored the adventures of Tom Sawyer, so we wanted to create our own.

We would normally light a fire to warm ourselves whilst in the bush and at times sniff thinners solvent, drink a little opaque beer if we had some, but mostly puff cigarettes that would have been brought by Patrick whose father worked for a cigarette manufacturer and sent him cigarette bricks for the teachers which never found their way to the teachers, as we smoked some and sold what we could to secondary and other students.

On one occasion whilst in the bush, we heard some movement in the dark, and we urged whomever was in the dark to come forward or risk a mob beating (huruweki), and from the dark emerged adult fellow donning a leather sun hat exclaiming that these a young boys being mischievous in the middle of the night, back into the dark. Another of his compatriot also emerged from the dark and we quickly observed them to be armed. We had never seen a fighter, and only romanticized about being a fighter for freedom.

But we really did not think we were ever going to be fighters coming from black middle class families, we were more likely never going to come back to this school after we graduate primary level for the same reason, that these bush fighters (comrades to the majority of the black population and terrorists to the existing regime) had now pushed the boundaries of their fight just under 70km from the heart of the capital.

We were more likely to be conscripted into the Rhodesian Army or sent overseas into exile than we were to join the guerillas, the ranks were swelled with recruits from the rural areas. My uncles AP Ndoro had been an activist with the internal settlement black politicians with the ousted founding president of Zanu, Ndabaningi Sithole, and during school holidays we would wear T-Shirts with adorned with Sithole's face because they were given out for free.

We were instructed to go and get some respectable secondary school boys to come and have a chat with them. A friend of mine Tapiwa Mtetwa, a member of the game named "Danger Perigo", had a giant of a brother who was feared even though he was in form 3 is I remember well, nicked-named Jab Mtetwa, for the potential jab you may get from him. So, we had no doubt who we were going to arouse from his sleep to have these conversations, we were to wait in the sidelines whilst they discussed, after which we were instructed to go wake up all the boys' primary dormitories to assemble in the church, eventually the whole school was assembled in the church.

More of the armed men emerged from the bush, some were intoxicated or drinking brandy, but others one could not help but observe that they were extremely alert to the point of paranoia. Two things that they were most concerned (1) being identified by a pupil (2) potential for an attack and escape routes out of the church into the bush.

A pungwe (night vigil) filled with political education by one of them called a political commissar began, which was punctuated by the exaltation of the Zanu PF military and political leadership, denunciation of internal settlement leadership particularly "Ian Douglas Smith and Abel Muzorewa" by full names, whilst explaining reasons for sustaining the guerilla warfare and occasional motivational singing.

This was the first of two such sessions ever held in my memory. Some senior students who were completing their senior year at the school being O Level are reputed to have left with the fighters after their final exams or before. I know that Tapiwa Rushesha who later became a friend was said to have joined the struggle as it was termed from this school, I later meant him at karate HQ several years later and was married to Oppah (now Oppah Muchinguri – Senior Zanu PF senior figure).

Salisbury to Park Meadowlands-1979

I had been invited to take the entrance exam at St Ignatius, but when I arrived at our new home, I was told that I would enrol at Cranborne Boys' High School where my cousin Shongwe had enrolled in the last term of 79 transferring from Waddilove secondary school form 1 to Cranborne. My first day at Cranborne, I was selected to attend cricket training for under 14, since I was a year older, my English both written and speaking were so limited that I did not even hear the intercom announce my name, so I did not attend neither did I know what cricket was.

The following morning, I was asked to go see the head teacher, upon being asked why I did not attend, the communication barrier was too much it was better to get two lashings, Clive Barns was the teacher, which felt like nothing given the kind of lashings we were used to at Waddilove. However, the next sessions I made sure I attended, I quickly made friends with

Tamuka Gonah and Farai Chiro, the two had been to multiracial primary schools and were fluent in spoken English, and they became my interpreters.

My first practice session in cricket was a disaster, the boys I joined were not happy that one of their own positions maybe be the target. They made me bat first after brief explanation and I went for it. It looked like baseball I had seen on television. When I hit the ball, it started spinning in the air and I followed it, thinking the object of the game was to keep hitting to deny those who want to get to it. I was called out for obstruction, and they had a good laugh, but by the end of the season I was in the team, I also made the rugby team and by sixth form was the fastest man in sprints and hurdles.

Harare 1982 – Greengrove

By form 3 I had changed schools, and was at Oriel Boys' High School, we had moved from Park Meadowlands and riding to Cranborne was just too much. We had moved to Greengrove, and I opted for Oriel, mainly cause Gonah had moved there several months before and I used to ride from Greengrove to his house to do a history project using his families encyclopaedia. At Oriel, I start meeting large numbers of exile children from USA and UK, I join basketball, which was just starting under a passionate student, Mike Sanyangore, Michael was American through and through, unafraid of authority and determined.

I was in class with Tafadzwa Gutu, now Doctor T Gutu, is brother was a form or so ahead of us, and they exhibited similar traits, bordering on bullying. I was to meet one of my best friends till today Siyayi Utete, a brilliant individual, who had lived his formative years in USA, we later followed each other to University of Zimbabwe doing Bsc General, dropped out and later Bachelor of Technology Honours Engineering.

Cause two schools drew students from these suburbs, Churchill mainly and Oriel marginally, my close friends in the suburb were from Churchill, some were distant relatives, the Mangoro Boys, the late Augustus and now Dr Charles Mangoro, but my closest friend was to be an ex-Oriel Boy I was introduced to by David Mandengenda, Kennedy Munyaradzi Javangwe. All these boys were academically scholarly compared to me, because of their friendship it helped me to sail through school.

This potential threat of being bullied at Oriel, at Cranborne I had fought and defeated both races of bullies in my age group in the bush after school at a place we aptly named kiddies' corner. Thanks to those boxing matches in the refugee camps in Rusape and a two-year stint at the school of hard knocks, Waddilove. Waddilove had taught me to stand-up to bullies, selectively, and to exact extreme revenge in the still of night to anyone who attempted to bully me or my friends or the weak, in what was called "huruweki" (whole works).

I joined Shukokai Karate Do, Karate Headquarters on Rezende Street, here over time I would make invaluable friendships which have lasted to today, it is here I met Pius Matambandzo, David Matipano, Herbet Muregerera, Kingston Dutiro and Julius Ncube among others too many to mention. Later in life I became the public relations officer of the Zimbabwe Karate Union.

At karate headquarters we punched and kicked faster and harder than any other club in Zimbabwe and we reigned supreme in tournaments, and this news made its way back into the Oriel and nightclubs. Thus, I escaped any bullying altogether including my friends no matter which school they went to.

By 1986, I made it to University of Zimbabwe, I had a mind of joining the Air Force so I could fulfil my childhood fantasy I used to share with my father which he thought unrealistic in Zimbabwe, a Military Coup. I was not even quite sure I wanted to join air force anymore, but yes, I made it to University Zimbabwe even with a hectic family business and sporting programme both at school and outside. I had become the school number one sprinter and hurdler. I always operated below the rudder of the teaching staff at high school except when receiving an unexpected academic award or other, and this will not be repeated as it put in the sites of the teaching staff.

1986, we entered University of Zimbabwe, and the University would never be the same again, within a short period I had been reunited with another childhood friend Marcos Makoni.

One night I objected to the boys harassing a lady I knew from Roosevelt at student's union and the hooligans thought they would have none of me. A fight broke out and I did not participate but, this fight was fought by persons who would later become my expanded allies, which made Marco to comment that I was a Warlord, and hence was born the crown warlord at University Zimbabwe.

Work Experience

After university I would work as a trainee manager in production at Trinidad Industries, a job I cajoled Mike Wakatama the MD, whom I had known when he came to lead and put together Zimbabwe Mining Development Corporation together with my father. The state enterprise itself the brainchild of Uncle Christopher Ushewokundze, who would come home and talk to my father about it over the dinner table. I later joined BP and Shell and quickly became Production Manager for the Willowvale Lubricants Plant, the highest-level manager at the facility. I then joined IDC Zimbabwe and worked as Executive Mineral Processing & Engineering, and technical advisor to the Minister of Industry, Dr Nathan Shamuyarira, I left IDC in January of 1999, joining International Finance Corporation and within three months I was moved to Johannesburg.

During my time as Minister's advisor, we persuaded him to open the fuel sector to everyone, and forced Minister Chikowore to announce that you could have an oil company if you had a 200-litre drum of fuel. I also persuaded him to put a time limit on the support to the South African auto-industry, and thereafter allow the import of Japanese cars.

Since my leaving IFC end of 2004, I have found several businesses in consulting, bank training and construction. The consulting and training businesses were very successful until the 2008 economic crisis which led to significant downscaling and restructuring as well as closure of the training businesses as our partners American company Omega Performance retreated from frontier markets. Seeing these winds of change and my assessment that the stimulus package by the government of South Africa will be in mega build projects, I sought to participate in this sphere.

I had to find an entry, and the opportunity arose when and old university and karate acquaintance Betram (Zaji) Zabane, of South African origins was awarded a mechanical installation package contract at the Medupi Power Station in Lepalele, Limpopo Province. Betram had been raised and educated in Zimbabwe with a Xhosa father married to a Black Rhodesian (Zimbabwean) woman. To all accounts he had been a brilliant fellow and graduated with an engineering degree later moving back to SA with the advent of democracy. However, he was to suffer a head injury that has left him with challenges with his short-term memory. So, during execution of the project, the client observed capacity problems for such a big installation and requested that he finds a project manager.

I dusted my CV gave it to another acquaintance, Leigh Dube, who had maintained a friendship with Zaji since University, Leigh had to vouch on my behalf to Zaji who was not fully convinced of my capabilities but took the chance anyhow based on the vouch and that at one time I was Sempai (assistant instructor) training him Karate.

Within a short space of time, I presented him with my evaluation and what needed to be down, and all doubts evaporated, and a friendship developed, now I had the credentials in construction. At the time of writing, I had moved to Papua New Guinea, this was in support of my spouse who found an opportunity to be on expatriate package after frustrations in corporate South Africa, from downright racism even more acute to a black person not of South African heritage and being skipped of promotions in favour of black Southern African origins. This was no different in the business field where President Zuma had promoted a fascism of a particular kind which excluded at its core all blacks who came from outside South Africa.

Chapter Six: The Zimbabwe Dream
By Tafi Chihota

The year was 1975, and I was six years old. Rudo my older sister was 10, and Kura, my brother was 3. We travelled as unaccompanied minors from London England to Lusaka, Zambia, where we were received by my mother's family, she being of the Bemba clan from Kasama, near the border with what was then called Zaire. Mum's younger brother, my uncle Gabriel welcomed us to his home in Kamwala where we were made to feel right at home and welcomed. It was to be a short visit, as we were in transit to Rhodesia.

My dad had been involved with the struggle for the liberation of his homeland since the government of Ian Smith had a Unilateral Declaration of Independence in 1965, cutting the umbilical cord with Britain. Baba was immersed in ZANU in Zambia with the late Herbert Chitepo being his main mentor.

In 1968, the year before I was born, pops was dispatched to Dar Es Salaam, Tanzania as the ZANU Representative. I was born in Dar and was given the name Pepukai by my father. On getting word that her son now had a son, my paternal grandmother back in Goromonzi, Rhodesia, sent a telex to Dar Es Salaam that my name be Tafirenyika, a somewhat heavy 11-character moniker which I struggle with to this day, which loosely translated means "we died for the country". The context was that she could not be with the first-born son of her firstborn son, because of the struggle against settler colonialism. In Rhodesia, in common with all known liberation activists and operatives, dad was a wanted man.

We lived in a shared apartment in Dar with Nathan and Dorothy Shamuyarira, he, being a lecturer at the local university, and she being a nurse at Aga Khan Hospital, where I was born. In 1972, on the advice and with the assistance of Uncle Nathan, dad got a scholarship to attend Morehouse College in Atlanta Georgia, and with his wife and three children in tow, we left for America.

On graduation from Morehouse, dad then enrolled at the Inns of Court, in London England to pursue a law degree. During this transition, mum and dad decided that the three existing children go to Zimbabwe for the summer, before returning and enrolling at school in England. The country was still known as Rhodesia, but that name was virtually forbidden to be uttered in our home, and we always only ever called the country Zimbabwe despite that name not existing on any map at that time.

Uncle Gabriel had one of the few television sets in Kamwala at the time, and I vividly remember his small sitting room being packed to the rafters with friends and neighbours crowded around the black and white TV set, watching Muhammed Ali fight George Foreman in Zaire, in the epic "Rumble in the Jungle". Those who couldn't be accommodated in the house, peered through the window to catch a glimpse of the spectacle. There were loud shouts and chanting as the fight progressed, and a great celebration as Alis hand was raised at the end of the fight, as the victor. This is my earliest African recollection, my warm welcome back to Africa.

We travelled by bus from Lusaka to Salisbury, accompanied by dad's cousin; babamukuru Lucas. From Salisbury, we took another bus into the nearby countryside, to Goromonzi, where my maternal grandmother and my uncles and aunts lived.

We arrived shortly after dark. When I say dark, I mean dark. The outline of the village of Yafele could only just be made out by the amber glow of the fires in the thatch and mud huts, fires.

that were used to cook meals, and around which families would gather and chat in the evening. Out of the darkness, a loud and excited cry of "vana va Lovemore vauya!!!" was let out. Within minutes, we were being carried at shoulder height by a swarm of people who, to my siblings and I, were absolute strangers. We were deposited at the entrance of a nearby hut, which I later realised, was my grandmother's kitchen.

My siblings and I spoke English with a curious Southern drawl, and between us we had a vocabulary of maybe one hundred words of the local language, chiShona. This was despite my parent's best efforts to make us fluent in our mother tongue whilst living in exile. The love that we were received with was unmistakable; it shone in the beaming faces that surrounded us, it translated clearly and there was no language barrier.

All I could see in the dim light of the smokey hut was smiling faces. We were squeezed with hugs and passed around from person to person, people whose faces we didn't know. In the morning we were awakened by the sound of a cockerel heralding the start of a new day. In the light of day we met, laughed, and communed with the family members who had met us at the roadside on the previous evening when we arrived on the bus. Until then, we had only been told that we came from a big family. In exile we only knew each other as the nuclear family, whereas in the village, I felt an immediate bond and sense of belonging and did my very best to squeeze out every last bit of chiShona that I possessed. Between my broken Shona and my extended family's limited English, we found a way to communicate. This was my introduction to Zimbabwe

The village had no plumbing, no running water, no electricity, and we would cross the road to go to ablutions at a place called pa "Community" where we would take showers and access flush toilets. I remember being handed a stone and being shown how to scrub the bottom of my feet to get them clean. Ambuya insisted on carrying the three-year old Kura on her back for most of the day, while I joined the team of boys whose job it was to tend to cattle. I learned how to use and crack a whip braided from the stripped bark of trees and attached it to a stick.

The experts amongst the boys could crack a whip and make it sound as loud as a gunshot. The boys made and used catapults which we would use to hunt doves and pigeons and Guinea fowl which in the evening would augment the meal. I was a useless shot, and a result I never hit anything.

Before the advent of cell phones and the Internet the only available mode of communication was by letter, and if you could access it, telex. The nearest post office was around a kilometre away from Gogo's homestead. One morning she told Rudo to put on her Sunday best dress (which was a powder blue lacey frock, complete with satin ribbons and all the trimmings). Rudo also put on her knee length sheer white stockings with patent leather shoes. I recall how her hair was braided and secured with powder blue satin ribbons. Gogo then had us accompany her to the post office, a twenty-minute walk down the country road.

I recall the postmistress being a stern, middle-aged white woman. Ambuya told us to talk with the postmistress and ask if Catherine Chimanikire had received any mail. Gogo dictated a telex to my dad back in England letting him know that we had arrived safely. I recall the intense curiosity and mild bemusement on the part of the postmistress at seeing the spectacle of my sister and hearing the spoken English that came out of her mouth. She asked a lot of questions about us and asked what England and America were like. She couldn't fathom how these little black African children who were staying in the village had travelled from abroad to visit family. She wasn't unfriendly, but her demeanour bugged me, in that it made me feel like we were anomalous curiosities on display, like monkeys grinding an organ.

That summer flew by so fast, and we returned to England. We were received by very excited parents and introduced to the latest member of our growing family. My youngest brother had been born in the time that we were away. My parents had bought a cassette tape recorder and asked us lots of questions about our journey. I can still hear my dad asking those questions "what did you see in Zimbabwe?".

"Who did you see in Zimbabwe?" "What do you think of Zimbabwe?" "What did you like about Zimbabwe?"

"What didn't you like about Zimbabwe?"

We lived in a two-bedroom flat in Regents Park and had long conversations over dinner and at the weekends on rainy days. The subject that always arose came to be known by us as "The Zimbabwe dream". Mum and Dad would talk to us about their dream for us to have a house and each of us children would chime in with the description of the dream house with four bedrooms, a swimming pool, and a tennis court. The house would be double storied and have a large garden with fruit trees and a rose garden and a rolling green lawn.

We collectively fantasized about our shared future back in the promised land of Zimbabwe this was The Zimbabwe dream. Having never been to Salisbury but having heard so much about it, mom's contribution to the Zimbabwe dream was to live in a residential area she had heard of an area called Mount Pleasant, a sight unseen. Mum was just enchanted by the name Mount Pleasant.

Shortly before independence in 1979, dad got his law degree. The political winds of change were blowing in earnest, and many who had been in the diaspora were now returning. Bishop

Abel Muzorewa was the Prime Minister of what was now known by the double-barrel name "Zimbabwe-Rhodesia".

When we first arrived in Salisbury, we were hosted for the first month or so at the home of my dad's cousin babamudiki Martin in Kambuzuma, one of the many townships set aside for urban black Rhodesian families. The house was small, the streets were dusty but we somehow managed to cram 2 full size families into that small 3 bedroomed house.

In short order Dad quickly found a job as an executive assistant to the chairman of one of the larger listed companies at the time and mom got a good administrative job at a local bank.

We moved from Kambuzuma into a rented house in an area called Waterfalls. It was a medium-sized house with a big yard, and I recall plucking granadillas and grapes straight off the vines in the backyard. The weekends were consumed either by visiting relatives or receiving them; "this is babamudiki so and so", we were told or "this is sekuru and ambuya so and so"2, and we were told where each was placed on the family tree.

I quickly realized that my family was ever so much bigger than that which we had been exposed to during our summer in Goromonzi a few years earlier.

The segregationist legislation that had governed who could live where along colour lines was repealed under the government of Bishop Muzorewa, which allowed blacks to acquire property in areas previously restricted to whites.

I remember how on one week during that time, mom and dad had been excited about something. As children, we didn't know what the excitement amongst our parents was, but we just knew that it was something big. When the weekend came around mom and dad piled us up in the newly acquired Peugeot 404 that he had as a perk from dad's work.

We drove to the north of Harare and pulled up at the gate of what seemed like a typical English Manor. A gardener came and met us at the gate which he proceeded to open. We drove down the driveway and were met by Mr. and Mrs. Bowles. Cursory introductions were made and then Mr. and Mrs. Bowles went and sat on lawn furniture under the shade of a tree and had tea. Mum led us into the house. "This is our new home guys", announced my dad.

It was a four-bedroom double story home with a swimming pool on the side and a tennis court in the backyard. There were fruit trees of every description ranging from apples and oranges to tangerines and nectarines, peaches and pears, more mulberry trees than we could count, all laden with fruit.

The house was surrounded by rolling grounds, with two acres of lawn. Barely able to contain ourselves we ran into the house and began allocating ourselves bedrooms.

My parents had just secured a mortgage, and concluded the sale agreement with the Bowles', who were now in the process of vacating the house, and we would be moving in on the 1st of the month mum told us. We were home. The Zimbabwe dream was no longer just a dream. It was now a reality.

Schools too had begun to be desegregated and people would go to schools within the zone of their residence. Kura and I were amongst the very first black students at Courteney Selous School in Greendale, three or four kilometres away from the new house in Mandara.

Our accents had now evolved into something akin to the English spoken in London, with our having spent the last four years there. We could understand chiShona well enough, but we didn't speak it with any degree of fluency or confidence. This set us apart from many of our fellow black students, creating an invisible division. I recall one student, who has been a friend from then until now, Frank Lupafya calling me "ngode ngezi" or "lover of white people".

He would say things like "koongfoo" for kung-fu, and "Yah Mah Ha" for Yamaha motorcycles, and I would laugh at his pronunciation.

Having been raised in a diverse and multicultural environment I had no trepidation with mixing and mingling with the white kids. People with names like John Fotheringham, Gerald McLaughlin, and Colin Nelson.

The girls I found easiest to talk to had names like Tracy Locke, Michelle Smith, and Olga Duran. People like Alice Nyagumbo and Kundai Gombe were more challenging for me to engage with. Franks family had recently moved to Mandara from Glen Norah, an all-black township, and I guess this was his first multicultural immersion.

He was dumbfounded and scandalized to see white ladies playing tennis on the school courts, bare legged wearing short tennis skirts with the puffy tennis knickers underneath which were in vogue at the time.

We made fast friends with people like Charles Mbanje and Pepukai Sanyangore, who were also recent returnees from abroad, themselves having previously lived in the US and the UK. The teaching staff at the school was all white and I recall names like Mrs. Drury, and Miss Bennett, Mr. Robinson, and Mr. Nash.

We played marbles every morning before the bell, and then again at break time, after collecting our daily ration of Caramello (a delicious milk chocolate drink made by Dairibord at the time) and wolfing down sandwiches brought from home. Fights were common, but the school came up with what in retrospect, was a bizarre way of conflict resolution. It was called "Gloves", and Gloves were held every Friday after school.

Gloves involved the two protagonists putting on oversized boxing gloves, and under the supervision of a teacher, would have at it with each other until one yielded, or both retired in exhaustion. Most fights were between black and white boys, never any girls.

The walls of the hall where the fights took place would be lined by spectators to the gladiation, jeers and cheers would ring out. When the fight was done, win, lose or draw- the combatants would be compelled to shake hands to demonstrate that the 'beef' was over. Done and dusted. A few hours later, the same hall would be the venue every Friday for "film shows", where a movie was played from a reel onto a screen from a rattling projector. This marked the official start of the weekend.

On the school holidays the white kids and their families would head off "down South" and go to the beaches of Durban, Port Elizabeth and Cape Town, and after the holidays they would come to school laden with treasures of exotic candy not found in Zimbabwe; candy like Bubble Yum and Popping Sherbert, which they would show off to those of us whose movement was still restricted by Apartheid- an institutionalized segregation which saw those of our colour prohibited from enjoying the many pleasures of South Africa. Curiously my white fellow students identified themselves as "European" whilst calling us blacks "Africans".

I remember asking them questions like "you were Rhodesian now you are Zimbabwean, but you still call yourself European? How, when neither Rhodesia nor Zimbabwe are in Europe… so how can you be European?" I don't recall ever getting a satisfactory answer to this question, more than once the issue would be settled on a Friday afternoon by 'gloves'.

One Saturday morning I recall an irate white man banging on the gate of our house. Followed by, me, dad went to the gate to see what the problem was. "Boy, go and call your baas" demanded the white man. At that time (and despite their ages) all gardeners were referred to as "boy", whether 'garden boy' or 'houseboy' whilst female domestic workers were known as "house girls" and "maids".

"Which boss do you want me to call?" my dad had replied…. The white man replied: "The owner of the house you bloody kaffir!"

"You are speaking to the owner of the house" my dad replied in a deadpan monotone, "and I will call the police to remove you if you don't leave immediately." I saw the grasp dawn on the face of the irate white man as he realized that we were now in a very new era where the status quo of the past was giving way to a new reality.

His face went from red to a deathly pale, and he turned on his heels and marched off, never revealing the reason for his visit. We had a comfortable middle-class lifestyle with the vestiges of the old Rhodesia. Mom would buy milk coupons of different coloured round plastic tokens that resembled large coins. Each colour (which denoted a product from the milk float), made its rounds in the suburb every morning even before the birds began chirping.

There were coupons for full cream milk, skimmed milk, fat free milk and so on. The milk was so good that it tasted like mildly sweetened ice-cream. The full cream milk was non homogenized and, through the clear glass bottle you could see a 10 centimetre thick layer of cream at the top of the bottle, and you'd have to shake it to get an even mix of cream and milk.

Every day, by 6:00 o'clock AM the following morning the coupons which would have been placed on the ground outside the gate during the previous evening, would have magically transformed into one litre bottles of milk, in thick glass bottles, which were reusable in a time long before "recycling" was a thing, and they were securely sealed with a cap made of tinfoil. Similarly, orders would be placed with Lobels Bakeries to a bakery employee who had a bicycle drawn bread cart, and there would be bread delivered to the gate well before 7:00 AM every morning, in rain and in sunshine.

In the years that I witnessed this system, I don't ever recall hearing of a single milk coupon going missing from the gate nor a bottle of milk being unaccounted for, the milk and bread which you ordered was invariably the milk and bread which you received.

Another random remnant of the Rhodesian era was the 'utility meter readers. These were workers of the state-owned companies responsible for electricity and water, and they wore orange overall or work suits and were invariably of "coloured" race, which is to say, they were of mixed black and white ancestry.

They were all men, and they attended to their duties on motorcycles and carried data forms on clipboards. They would ask for access to the electrical and water meters at every house, and they would write down the numbers indicated for the generation of monthly utility bills. This job was done exclusively by "coloureds3 and I don't recall ever seeing a black or white meter reader. I assume that the authorities at the time thought the job to be above the competency of blacks, and a grade of labour beneath the dignity of whites.

Another notable characteristic of our weekends was hosting and being invited to "braais" (barbecues and pool parties) where we would mix and mingle with fellow black families who had found themselves in situations of new found privilege. We would go to the Muzanenhamos, the Murerwas, the Zamchiyas and the Kuparas, Maponderas and Vambes and Nyagumbos. Alternatively, they would come over to our home and we would have braais while playing in the pool and others playing tennis all day. Our dads would drink sherry, whiskey, and brandy with coke whilst our moms consumed Green Valley and Mukuyu wine, or Cinzano Bianca and sherry. This was our new reality; a reality that had been inconceivable even a short few years prior, we all, young and old, revelled in the excitement of the birth of the new reality called Zimbabwe, and we were pregnant with optimism and expectations for the halcyon days that we knew lay ahead.

I can't recall her name, but there was a ginger-haired white girl who lived nearby at a house across the vlei from ours. The vlei offered a venue for boisterous boys' "expeditions" as my brother and I would call them; where we find crabs in the stream that ran through it, tortoises, and the occasional duiker. All alone, this girl who didn't go to the same school as us, but was around my age of 12, wondered around our "expedition vlei" and was every inch a tomboy.

We struck up a friendship, and in no time, we were visiting each other's homes. She would come and climb trees with us at the house and we would all make a mess of ourselves and food fight with mulberries, staining our hands and clothes with

Mulberry juice. At times we would go to her house where we would play for a while. One day her mother, who I hadn't yet met until then, arrived home and found me playing in her backyard. She immediately asked me who I was, then told me to go home. She followed me home and asked to meet my parents.

To my mom, she came across as civil but curious. She introduced herself and having made the connection of our friendship with her daughter, my mom invited her to sit with her on the veranda and share a cup of tea. My friend's mom was in two minds, and obviously had never encountered a situation where she would socialize as "equals" in an Africans home. She and my parents sat and sipped tea with fresh homemade scones with whipped cream and strawberry preserve, on the veranda. Having broken the ice, the three of them began what would be a long and heartfelt conversation with mom and dad telling them about their participation in the liberation movement that brought about the independence of Zimbabwe. The white lady explained how she had lost her husband four or five years earlier while on duty when he served in the Rhodesia Light Infantry on Border Patrol and had been shot dead by terrorists. Seeing her child who had lost her father in a war waged against people like us, now frolicking and playing with the children of the enemy, brought about profound mixed emotions in her.

Why did my husband have to die? What did he die for? These were the rhetorical questions she was posing to my parents, questions which they couldn't answer. She was obviously going through her own personal transition within the context of the transition of the country from Rhodesia to Zimbabwe

Over the next couple of years, the largely white suburbs and their white 'Group A' public schools began to have more and more black families and fewer and fewer white students. The white families where "taking the gap" and emigrating to apartheid South Africa or the lily-white shores of Australia and New Zealand. New and old private schools had an upsurge in new white enrolment. A few families moved to England.

All those uprooting and relocating, were doing so to places where the people in charge were white. They couldn't come to terms with being governed by black people. They are the same people who moved from South Africa to 'Oz' and 'Kiwi' land around the time the ANC assumed power in Afrique du Sud, LOL!

This is but a very brief account of my lived experience over the period of transformation between the death of Rhodesia and the birth of Zimbabwe. It was a time of growth and learning and experiencing the brunt of white racism and bearing the brunt of being ostracized by fellow blacks who looked just like me. I feel humbled and privileged to have lived through that period of historical significance and remain ever grateful to those who made it possible.

Chapter 7: Township Life vs. Afrikan Identity

By Unathi Mbolekwa (Nyathi)

Even though I cannot claim full "township credentials" since I only lived in Diepkloof, Soweto, Johannesburg, South Africa, for the first few months of my infancy. I do however believe an underestimated number of urban "black Southern Afrikans" were affected by "township life" in some way or another.

It is evident that a majority of black Afrikan people lost much of their identity and heritage to colonisation, which came with a "ghetto lifestyle" that emerged in townships built for them during the late colonial era.

I have therefore come to appreciate the importance of identity as it provides a sense of gravitas; hence, identity is a sensitive political and cultural topic. For these reasons, colonisation deliberately disrupts identity by tampering with values or standards, which are cornerstones for self-determination. Without standards, the colonised become disorderly and incapable of shaping and upholding social cohesion.

Disrupting the relatively peaceful and free homestead life of pre-colonial Afrika to restricted townships was effective in destabilising black societies. Living under oppressive laws in low-cost housing under crowded conditions created frustration, shattering the moral compass of black Southern Afrikans for generations.

In my humble view, the radical changes that came with colonisation resulted in a curious dilemma for black southern Afrikans: having to navigate life by juggling between two very different and often opposing "value systems".

The drastic transition from Afrikan homestead life to living in restricted westernised townships, which my parents experienced and exposed me to, through regular visits to both - made me notice a type of confusion in values and ethics that many black Southern Afrikans still struggle with, even after attaining independence.

To make sense of the confusion, I attended an African culture school to study the Principles and Ethics of African culture and identity from an Afrikan perspective. It is from this Afrikan angle and personal experiences; that I aim to highlight some of the challenges and triumphs faced by many black southern Africans during the crossover from the late colonial era to liberation.

For me, it began with something that at first seemed unrelated to colonisation, in regards Afrikan identity and culture.

Culturally speaking my first name, Nkosinathi means King-with-us, Nkosi-na-thi and is normally given to a firstborn son, to signify an heir within the family line. Something similar exists for first-born girls, but religiously Nkosinathi can also imply God is with us by being blessed with a firstborn son for family legacy, so to speak. "God-with-us" biblically translates to the name Emmanuel.

Shortened to Unathi or U-na-thi, which in this case translates to He-with-us, the letter "h" stresses the letter "i", so it is pronounced Unati with a strong "i" at the end. I was told Nkosinathi was shortened to Unathi to accommodate our English colonisers who still mispronounced it.

Preferring Europeanised names like Emmanuel, the church was not pleased with baptising me Unathi, ironically finding the name not Christian enough. However, my mother stood firm and refused to change my name any further!

Upon reflection, my name had already been influenced by colonisation to align with the Christian "God" who is depicted as a white Caucasian male with a Eurocentric persona, much like the church, which discouraged Afrikan values and culture.

The less colonial understanding of the "Creator" in black Southern Afrikan culture might be better understood as MoYah. A single genderless, parentless spirit energy that powers and permeates, as everything, throughout the eternal infinity, thus cannot be represented in any shape or form. Sounds more like scientific spirituality than a faith-based religion.

This is quite different to the Christian deity claimed to be some or all of the above, yet portrayed as a male (father) in heaven, represented by the concept of a Trinity. God the father, god the Holy Spirit and god the son, who has a mother known as Mary mother of god, along with idols, statues and images that, represent them.

The impulse to accommodate European standards at the expense of Afrikan principles is of great concern, especially in independent Afrika. It is a mental after effect of colonisation that uses Afrikans to automatically undermine and erase their own well thought out spiritual identity without fully realising the self-defeat.

During colonisation, most issues to do with Afrika were disregarded, mismanaged and cheapened to give the impression that the continent and its black inhabitants and culture are insignificant. Many black people were misnamed or just renamed in the same way as Afrikan territories, queendoms, kingdoms, and empires. Countless monuments of Afrikan heritage were changed or condemned and converted into churches to diminish their true importance.

Millions of black Afrikans were forced from their well-organised, fertile and mineral-rich lands where they had survived for centuries, carrying out productive activities such as; environmentally friendly architecture, organic agriculture and chemistry, mining and metal technology, astrology, astronomy, mathematics and international trade.

Thousands of communities and families were dispassionately divided and split apart to end up working as cheap or slave-type labour in white farms and mines on land stolen from them.

The "carving" or "scramble for Afrika" at the Berlin Conference in 1884-5 that split indigenous territories and communities on a tribe, homestead and even family basis was a devastating tool of "divide and rule."

Indigenous populations had to find ways to survive certain ruin, further eroding Afrikan identity. Afrikan social cohesion was damaged and expunged from public knowledge while the revered home-grown principles of "Ubuntu" were almost forgotten.

The harm caused by missionaries and colonial administrations supported by military force, violated the "live and let live" ethics of Ubuntu. Colonial education instilled long-term effects of black inferiority on the Afrikan psychology.

With little space to manoeuvre, a "bible in the left hand and a gun in the right," black people in Southern Afrika were forced to accept that, which made little sense regarding their oppression condoned by a new religion and social order.

In search of work to make a living in urban areas, many black Southern Afrikans moved into towns being built into westernised cities with backbreaking labour under the stringent conditions of colonial masters.

Meanwhile, black labourers lived in small "servant's quarters" or informal settlements, also known as squatter camps, often located close to smoky, unhealthy, and polluted industrial sites till today. Compounds and hostels were more common for black miners.

Demand for black urban housing increased, leading to specific areas being designated along racial lines, resulting in the forced removal of people of colour to underserved locations on the outskirts of expanding towns and cities.

It is these compounds and squatter camps that appear to have evolved into satellite "locations" and/or "townships," which became the primary residence for black southern Africans.

The negative impact of densely populated and inadequately serviced townships became obvious. Urban black people began to realise the extent of their drawback owing to oppressive policies of racial discrimination and apartheid disguised as "Separate Development".

Black townships became a time bomb, ticking towards an explosion of social degradation. A pressure outlet from the stifling conditions was inevitable. As the morals of black people in townships fell, crime rose. Yet, something else in the air started to change.

In what had begun centuries earlier as homestead resistance against colonisation grew into Afrikan queendoms, kingdoms and empires fighting against outside domination. Resistance against outside domination intensified into full-blown liberation movements, which crept into the new urban homesteads called townships.

An attitude adjustment in township people brought out a new breed of Afrikan, finding identity in urban settings. This new Afrikan came with makeshift drums, tin guitars, and jazzy penny whistle rifts mixed with traditional Afrikan rhythms and lyrics to express the blues of oppression and hardship.

Infused with western influences, "ghetto blues" took over southern Afrika with almost telepathic precision, bursting into a creative rainstorm. True township culture took hold of the Afrikan psyche and land scape and southern Afrikas urban social scene would never be the same again.

The new breed of Afrikan was streetwise, with a revolutionary type swagger of fortitude, and somewhere there, is where my exposure to township life began through storytelling and periodic visits.

Exposure to township life

My mother and her siblings were orphaned young and as per culture they were taken in by their late mother's sister, who was married, but childless. My mother and her siblings automatically adopted their aunties married surname.

Determined to make something of herself, my mother left her homestead in the Eastern Cape province of South Afrika after school to start training as a nurse at none other than Baragwanath Hospital in the bustling township of Soweto in the late 1950s.

As the story goes, my mother like many other black people at the time got involved in the urban resistance against Apartheid. At some point in 1963, she went to visit a relative in the then neighbouring country of Southern Rhodesia, which was also going through its own type of apartheid and white minority rule.

Rhodesia is where my mother met my father, but only realised she was with child after returning to South Afrika. Diepkloof, in Soweto, is consequently, where I lived for my first few months. I automatically inherited my mother's adopted surname because my father lived in Rhodesia.

Less than a year after my birth, my mother had to leave South Afrika again, to avoid the ruthless internal security due to her involvement in the resistance against apartheid. It was not safe for her to remain in South Afrika; however, the move was not to be that simple.

Like her aunty, my mother adopted two of her elder sister's daughters from the East London Township of Mdantsane. Living in Mdantsane proved difficult for my mother's elder sister, who had children with one of those slick, sweet-talking, well dressed "township boys" of old, who for whatever unfortunate reasons was not very present.

With the three of us my mother travelled through Botswana into the Caprivi Strip (now known as the Zambezi Region) to enter the newly independent country of Zambia in 1964. I am told the journey was challenging. We spent several nights in the wilderness before being collected and transported to Ndola, a quaint mining town where we lived as political exiles in a small townhouse.

Fast-forward a few years, my mother met another gentleman from Southern Rhodesia who was also living as a political activist in Zambia. They got married, and with the arrival of two more children, a move to a more spacious house in the suburbs of Ndola was pragmatic.

The new marriage meant that my surname changed to my stepfather's, although the surname on my birth certificate remained that of my mother's adopted maiden name. Zambia is an amazing country with hospitable people, going out of their way to support unliberated neighbouring Afrikans. In those days, the spirit of pan Afrikanism across the continent was profound.

From exile to war

Fast-forward another few years to 1977, my stepfather, driven by an instinct to return home after years of being away, made a family decision to move to Rhodesia, as the signs of imminent independence from white minority rule were apparent.

Sure enough, since the laws in Rhodesia did not allow black people to live where ever they wished, we stayed at my stepfather's, younger brother's house in a township called Mufakose in the then capital city of Salisbury, which would become Harare.

Like my stepfather, his younger brother grew up in their homestead of Chivi in Masvingo Province and with ambition moved to the city to find the type of education and success he desired.

I was on the cusp of becoming a teenager and recall Mufakose township as rather daunting. We were cautioned not to leave the house unless accompanied by someone familiar with the area until people got to know us, because that might cause unnecessary attention.

It was a tense political period in Rhodesia; I could feel the tension in the air was different to Zambia. Rhodesian forces were merciless towards black people and townships were urban hotspots of political friction. Furthermore, lethal reprisals to fellow black people found to be sell-outs or informants to the oppressive Rhodesian regime were not unheard of.

Similar reprisals upon sell-outs or informants were also not uncommon in the village homesteads and countryside where a gruesome "guerrilla bush war" for independence was taking place.

All of this reminded me of the stories my mother used to tell about her experiences in Soweto during the 1950s and early 1960s. It was essential to know one's surroundings because things could go very wrong, very quickly. Aimlessly wandering around in townships was never advisable.

While my stay in Mufakose was short, it was impactful. After that my visits to townships in Rhodesia until independence to Zimbabwe in 1980, though often brief, became frequent enough for me to notice that the township, perhaps like any other ghetto was not to be taken lightly.

Even though I had lived with political alertness in Zambia, it seemed the rules of engagement in the township were more direct and confrontational. This truth became clear to me during my next series of experiences in townships, especially when my mother decided to return to her home in South Africa, 16 to 17 years after leaving to enter exile.

My mother had a new Zimbabwean passport and surname so there was little chance of being detected by the apartheid security that was still in place. Soon after Zimbabwe gained independence in 1980, the entire family, with the exception of my stepfather, made the trip to my mother's South Afrikan homestead in 1981.

Due to the long distance between Harare, Zimbabwe, and my mother's village in the Eastern Cape, the trip had to be broken into two segments. The midway point was Johannesburg, and Soweto was where my mother had relatives that we could stay with.

It was nostalgic for mom to be back in South Afrika. We stayed at her cousin's house, which just so happened to be a popular Shebeen called the "Fish Pond" in an area of Soweto known as Dube.

Of course, the rules of engagement were to first move around with someone from the area so people get to know you and only then venture out "bit by bit." Luckily, Shebeens were and remain social spots where people in the "hood" come to buy their favourite beverages, with alcoholic liquor being the main one.

Since township culture has that strong sense of community, Shebeens are like holy-ground, where people of all types come to unwind and "let loose," as an escape from the often congested living conditions.

My auntie's house in Soweto was like most others in the township, typically four-roomed, known as "matchbox" houses. Matchbox houses in South Afrikan townships are practically identical to township houses in Zimbabwe and even Zambia often with a separate toilet in a small outside building, which I found convenient in the crammed surroundings.

The Shebeen closed down around 10 or 11 p.m., especially on weekends. We would transform the couch into a bed and use any spare mattresses and cushions to create additional sleeping spaces on the floor in the areas between the bedroom, dining room, lounge, and kitchen. Only to be woken up as early as 7 or 8 in the morning by customers looking to cure their hangovers with more alcohol for breakfast!

Even though Shebeens were originally illegal, many had become legal business entities, and the Fish Pond had a reputation of being "old skool," catering to a more mature crowd that liked listening to - you guessed it - blues and jazz.

South Afrika and, to a slightly less degree, Zimbabwe have a rich jazz and afro-jazz culture deeply rooted in township life. So, the selection of music at my aunties' Shebeen was always top-notch! Something smooth and intellectual was always playing in the background.

The "Old Skool Township Cats," as they were and are still affectionately known, many of whom were loyal Fish Pond patrons, were characteristically sharply dressed in shiny shoes and clean, ironed clothes with cross bands holding up baggy turn-up trousers. Classic!

The depth of musical knowledge the Old Skool Cats had and were willing to share to educate the younger generation about this rich township subculture, always impressed me.

South Afrikan jazz enthusiasts are not to be underestimated. The most unassuming of Old Skool Cats would enlighten on sounds, instrument-playing techniques and subgenres of music that I certainly never knew existed. It was truly awesome.

This rich communal township culture was nonetheless, juxtaposed to the horrifying reality that things could go very wrong in a matter of minutes. Especially in the days of apartheid when brotherhood could turn into brotherly bloodshed over something as trivial as accidently spilling a bit of beer, or brandy on someone's shoes.

Life was cheap for black people in South Afrikan townships during oppression. Dangerous and life-threatening crimes were discussed almost casually, awakening me to the reality of township life that my mother had cautioned me about.

Needless, to say, I witnessed many crimes over the years of visiting Soweto, particularly while doing the rounds with my elder cousin, the son of my aunty, the Fish Pond owner. I often found myself participating in goings-on I would rather forget, but that was just part of township life at that time.

In Mdantsane Township, I had yet another elder cousin (son to my mother's elder sister) who was also active in the underground movement against Apartheid. While being a good employee for Mercedes-Benz he had a reputation for being the first to strike in retaliation of danger, yet the sweetest guy you've ever met, until crossed.

like most townships during that period, being seen with my elder cousin in Mdantsane had huge advantages, but that did not help much when, on one occasion, his younger brother had to violently stop some random guy from stabbing me on the street in broad daylight. The attack happened as we made our way home from a local store, simply because the guy did not recognise me from the hood!

One evening, on a bus returning to the area where my elder cousin in Mdantsane lived, I remember finding a bloodstained Okapi flick knife on the floor next to where I sat. I cannot say why I picked it up, but in my young, naïve thinking, carrying a knife or gun was half-expected for a young black man living in a South Afrikan township.

That very evening, when I had the opportunity, I showed my older cousin the bloody knife I had found. He was not impressed, but in a calm and controlled voice, asked me to dispose of it as quickly and far away as possible. I complied promptly.

In hindsight, it could easily have been me who was a victim of that Okapi knife on the bus or on the day my younger cousin intervened to save me from a very probable stabbing.

As the years went by, I came to appreciate some underlying connections between my different experiences in Southern Afrikan and Zimbabwean villages and townships that I started visiting more and more regularly. People generally always try to have your back!

With these experiences, I noticed that despite poverty and strife, which came with an element of danger in desperation, the township also fostered a buzzy vibe of camaraderie and a sense of community, but most of all, a drive to succeed.

Although generally safer and cleaner with better service when compared, suburbs are more controlled with almost self-inflicted boredom. The sheer range and extent of possible social interactions that one can experience in townships is much richer than in affluent suburbs.

Practically everyone in the "hood" is as good as invited merely by hearing about or walking past your party. This open-door policy is something that rarely, if ever, happens in higher-end suburbs. The open-door policy of communal oneness in townships comes from Afrikan village life and homestead culture.

Accordingly, it is a bag of mixed emotions for me because, as a black person growing up in Southern Afrika, the township showed me crazy amounts of fun in the most poor and unexpected areas, where people of all races are welcomed, even during the "dark days" of Apartheid. Conversely, I cannot shake the sad reality that both my elder cousins from Mdantsane and Soweto perished in brutal and wasteful ways in or due to township life.

Even with all the contradictions and challenges, so many achievers have come from the township to become super influential, precisely for being streetwise and driven. How then does one reconcile these vivid contrasts of township life as an outsider or even from within?

How has the southern Afrikan "live and let live" identity of Ubuntu been affected by townships, especially during the broader crossover period? Well, I am sure the answers are as many as the questions, but what happened in Soweto after the fall of Apartheid and South Afrikan independence in 1994 is noteworthy.

So-We-To is an abbreviation for "South Western Townships" and currently proudly stands as one of the safest and celebrated spaces in South Afrika from practically being a war zone. And further to that, surrounded by a country whose crime statistics leave much to be desired.

Out of control political violence and crime drove the township spirit of the people in Soweto to surface after independence and make a stand to say, "No more, enough is enough"!

In typical township style, the people of Soweto took a stance to clean up and rid their streets of crime becoming a beacon of hope as to what is possible by coming together for the right reasons, compared to waiting for someone else to solve the problems.

As I stand to be corrected, it was what the people of Soweto stood for and did that made the authorities sit-up and take notice and responsibility, not the other way round as some may think.

Regrettably, in the same way the negative legacy of Apartheid lingers on in many South Afrikan townships - Zimbabwean townships are also in a state of contradiction between good neighbourliness and the ever-present possibility of instability.

Poverty and ailing services in crowded living conditions as a carryover of the colonial era are what drives crimes of desperation to become more frequent and sadly somewhat normalised.

The question then becomes: was it purely the more modern township attitude or the more ancient morals of Afrikan Ubuntu that drove the initiatives to bring a semblance of safety and stability to Soweto, or perhaps a combination of the two forces of good coming together?

Whatever it is, I hope Soweto can remain an example of how to improve the living standards of the large populations that live in high-density areas and townships across Afrika if not the world over.

Summary

After leaving Zambia and moving to Rhodesia, I attended a politically charged "black-conscious" school called Goromonzi High and then did an apprenticeship, qualifying as a Journeyman mechanic soon after Zimbabwe gained independence.

Coincidentally, I found employment at Mercedes-Benz Zimbabwe, known as Zimoco, and yes, German engineering and precision were quite the experience!

In between all of that I worked as a semi-professional dancer and choreographer, cabaret show artist, fashion model, part time art crafts and music promoter, small scale gold and emerald miner and kiosk trader, import and export as well as a partner in a gem cutting and jewellery making company. I think the word for that is "hustler".

Whether working as a technician or as a small to medium size entrepreneur with experience in the arts and a passion for innovation, Afrikan culture as my identity has always played an important role in my life, especially in "trying times" and in finding lasting solutions.

Having being exposed to various fields and disciplines and how they can be applied for better quality of life has shown me that flexibility, even within strict requirements is not a contradiction as many tend to believe. In fact, given the platform, different approaches can complement each other elegantly, particularly for that powerful process called critical-thinking.

In my modest opinion, many Afrikan leaders seem to have been conditioned to think unoriginally. Perhaps limited by a colonial hangover, Afrika's leaders do not seem to recognise that the true and real wealth of Ubuntu in action starts with and is all about critical Afrikan thinking.

The centuries-old grip that held Afrika down began to loosen in the 1950s, all the way to the 1990s, when country after country gained independence. However, this era also marked a time when many Afrikans celebrated their newfound freedom without fully recognizing that it was part of a broader pattern of mental dependence that persisted.

The solutions that Afrika's leaders do not seek, are perhaps, more often based on flexibility within context of local knowledge systems and not in external solutions from the ex-coloniser, as too often appears the case. Flexibility within the already none ridged frame of Ubuntu and its powerful potential is lost to a lack of critical Afrikan thinking.

The most important lesson learnt from the township was the welcoming attitude for open-minded dialogue, where talent and home-grown genius are allowed to flow as opposed to being stifled by political rhetoric, red tape and religious dogma.

Perhaps we cannot paint all townships with one brush or one with all, but that does not mean we cannot nourish as many with the right amount of colour to beam as beautiful as possible. The talent is abundant!

Looking forward; In 2007, half of the world's population was estimated to be living in urban areas. Could the township experience have some viable options to offer for high-density urban living?

Population growth and pollution are severe issues that demand immediate attention. Unfortunately, practical solutions are often, ignored due to political arrogance and corruption. Either way, it is important to comprehend the primary causes to prepare and evolve in order to secure the environment for our future.

The township experience of Southern Afrika may provide some compelling data and methods of approaching the housing problem for millions worldwide, avoiding densely populated areas from turning into a time bomb of social degradation.

Employing all available information from learnt experiences may help in addressing matters of population growth, as major problems such as affordable, sustainable urban shelter are not going anywhere any time soon.

Maybe, just maybe, somewhere between the ancient Afrikan philosophies and the streetwise township, solutions for managing high-density residences already exist on the continent of human origins.

From a personal point of view, I have two official adopted surnames while my cultural surname is not official. My first name was compromised to comply with foreign values stripping me of both my Afrikan as well as individual identity. Trust me when I say I understand "identity crisis" and cannot begin to explain the social and legal costs of it.

Thanks to exposure to my Afrikan homestead roots and guided township experiences, I developed a default setting that kept me sane enough to share these humbling, yet priceless experiences of knowledge gained.

Had my parents not allowed me access to my ancient heritage, I do not think I would have truly appreciated how Afrikan identity has transformed through a remarkable township experience, yet adhering to the original principles and wisdoms that shine light on the future.

My township experiences have been like a roller-coaster ride, opening my mind to the great potential that lies within my original Afrikan culture. These experiences have shown me that with a little perseverance and the right exposure, I too can stand up to say "No more! Enough is enough!"

These experiences and lessons have however taught me something more valuable than just saying it, but saying it in a way that the authorities will stand up to provide proper support because if they do not, it is also them on the line. After all, we will all end up breathing polluted air and drinking disease-infested water if we do not listen to the facts.

Southern Afrikan townships are like universities and are therefore an important part of the global black experience and history that can inform how social change can be better handled. Perhaps this is the beginning of a new and eye-opening chapter for modern black history, culture, and identity, but most importantly, from an Afrikan perspective, for without roots, how to bear fruits?

I acknowledge MoYah and ubuNtu passed down from our Afrikan ancestors. I also salute to the Afrikan Queens for initiating this project with "Township Girls".

Heitadha!!!

*Please note the author consciously chooses to use the spelling Afrika with a "k" as opposed to the more Anglicized "c".

Chapter Eight: Township Music- My First Love!

By John Matinde

"Music was my first love, and it will be my last;
The music of the future, the music of the past.
To live without my music would be impossible to do.
In these days of troubles, my music pulls me through ". (John Miles, 1976).

The story of my life is a bit of an odyssey. This hopefully will be an abridged account that focuses on why I identify myself as a "township boy", who had the privilege to be part of the crossover generation as Rhodesia transitioned to Zimbabwe.

It is respective, retrospective and indeed introspective.

By way of background, I was born in a little town called Essexvale (later renamed Esigodini, Zimbabwe). I'm a 20th Century boy... A second sibling born to an educationist mum and dad. Mum also rocks a medical background.

They were both strict disciplinarians who brooked no nonsense, and as dad progressed through the ranks to be Headmaster, he always believed we should live by example. In short, he reigned with the left, but ruled with the right. Dad's promotion in his career path saw us relocate to Bulawayo. My elder brother and I were to later return to that same school, Umzingwane, some 15 or so years later for our secondary schooling, as borders, following the two way split of that college into an academic stream, as well as an Agricultural Institute, relocated on new premises close the school farm, and renamed Esigodini Agricultural College).

So began an itinerant sojourn around Bulawayo Townships, firstly Mpopoma, then New Mpopoma, Old Luveve, New Luveve, and then back to Mpopoma, up till my dad was transferred to the Midlands (Zvishavane), where I only attended 5 school terms at primary, (and with it too all the formal Shona I ever studied), before going back to aforesaid Umzingwane for my secondary education.

Those Bulawayo days are my formative years, for my life experiences then, were to shape me forever, as I acquired crucial and critical life skills.

My love for music and listening to the radio started right there at Mpopoma, and my dad recognising this hobby, and to improve our English language comprehension skills, would often make my cousins and my siblings, listen to the radio news, and then go brief him on what we'd heard. No one knows why but all I usually did was mimic the radio presenter introducing news, too much family hilarity, and I'd leave it to the older guys to report the bulletins! (The formal class exercise as I recall was called ENGLISH COMPREHENSION, all part of the curriculum)!

Roll on a few years, and now at boarding school, after much protest from both my mum and him, I bribed them into getting me a portable radio to take to boarding school, after impressive exam results in Form 1, that I was indeed focused on my studies, my main argument being that after all every good boy (and girl) deserves favour. This was unprecedented at Mzingwane, as a portable radio had traditionally been the preserve of the school captain, but they generously (though strictly) stipulated which times I couldn't listen to my radio lest I distracted everyone! (Big mistake!!) (Younger readers, this was before the mobile phone had been invented).

I shall come back to my boarding school days...

Those of you who know the Bulawayo Townships I've mentioned, will agree they are as ghetto as they come. We as kids played and mingled with friends and school mates from very diverse backgrounds. Though regarded as privileged because of dad's status, we never looked at it that way.

My brother and I could be found clandestinely accompanying our motley crew of friends as they hustled for school fees and sustenance, selling various wares and foods in the "centrelines" (mukoto) between the houses and hedgerows, unfazed.

Merchandise was anything and everything, for pocket money as well as family sustenance. From sweets, boiled eggs, fruit, knitwear on behalf of their folks, we joined in. It was fun. It was their influence as well that introduced me to more diverse music than otherwise my parents allowed us to listen to on the radio. We'd often gather close to an illicit house- drinking party (shebeens) and enjoy watching patrons dancing to Smanje-manje music mostly by black South African artists like Izintombi ZesiManjemanje, Mahotella Queens, Soul Brothers, West Nkosi and many others. We may have even gate-crashed one or two concerts by these visiting artists, but I'm not saying...

And what was playing on the radio? Gospel music courtesy Kings' Messengers Quartet, Zim Choral from Epworth Theatrical Strutters (one of my late dad's favourite groups especially Kudzidza Kwakanaka i.e., Education is King!), pop music from the Beatles, Rolling Stones, Dave Clark Five, The Monkees; rock n' roll from Elvis Presley, Cliff Richard, Country music from Charley Pride and Jim Reeves... in fact the whole nine yards and then some! Lots of diverse music but with a heavy Western bias. One would argue, I was raised on rock. Rock music specifically, especially later in my teenage years, as I discovered 24-hour external music radio stations on the Short-Wave frequency, like the Maputo based LM Radio (Lourenco Marques, later renamed Maputo after Mozambique independence). More later...

In those Bulawayo days, Southern Rhodesia (as Zim was known then) enjoyed its own form of deeply practiced apartheid called segregation (by colour and ethnicity). This meant indigenous racial and mixed groups, could only live in designated areas, (blacks in townships, mixed heritage in their own minority suburbs, likewise Asians, with the "leafy" suburban houses exclusively reserved for whites.

This then meant "rich or poor" amongst us blacks, lived side by side in the hood, difference being on how big they'd extend or refurbish their houses, and what type of cars (imported or otherwise), they drove, if any. It might not seem likely to the younger reader that with unequal opportunities prevailing amongst races, we wouldn't have well-off people. But we did, and they also inspired many other ordinary folk to aim and strive very hard, for a better life, in the absence of Bank and large scale financial institutional support.

Right there along Block 21 in Mpopoma, just opposite the headmaster's house which we lived in (quite gentrified by government standards as was part of headmaster's pecks), lived Joseph Mtshumayeli, owner of the much famed red Pelandaba Buses which plied their trade around Matebeleland. He hailed from Kezi as I recall from the inscriptions that used to be de rigeur, blazoned on the bus doors then. When we arrived, he initially boasted about a dozen or so that he'd often park on the unbuilt vast undeveloped stands next to his end house, towards Nketa Drive. We knew they were about 12 because they'd all be numbered. By the time we left Mpopoma for the last time, headed for Gresham School in Zvishavane, he'd more than doubled his fleet of mostly DAF buses, which entertained and amazed everyone with their loud "whoosh" of state-of-the-art air brakes when they stopped! They were the epitome of luxury coaches way back then.

My dad must have also been inspired by Pelandaba's success, as he also became a bit of a motor fan on the side, simultaneously owning an unheard of two cars at a time by the time we relocated. I distinctly remember a large American Chevrolet was one of his fleet. He also owned an "Austin of England" estate car. So, I'm also into cars, and it's all entirely his fault…and I'm sticking to it!

And because a headmaster's salary alone could not sustain him and extended family, he started enterprisingly doing up trailers and scotch wagons from scratch, that we'd tow to my maternal grandad's farm, near Mashaba, or to our rural home near Pakame Mission, Shurugwi, and barter for livestock and grain. He'd keep most of the livestock and sell the excess to the Cold Storage Commission for slaughter, and the excess crop to the Grain Marketing Board.

This was the law of unintended consequences at play, for the Rhodesian regime, as it taught the marginalised not to just allow themselves to survive in poverty, but also to be enterprising and improve their lot, by themselves. It became a challenge for the ilk of my father, to prove their worth, not only to their peers, but also to the regime. Being a civil servant, they were barred from active politics. This only served to push those of a strong political persuasion like my dad, to join others secretly, as I recall many an evening, he'd disappear wearing his nationalist leather and feathered hat, to attend clandestine NDP political meetings, which then split into ZAPU and ZANU! Those memoirs I will leave for another day...

While at Mpopoma, my elder brother and I discovered there was a Youth Club that we could also join to pursue our various recreational pursuits. He was the sporty one, so it was soccer for him, and I naturally went the music way, learning to strum the guitar here and there, and discovered I was not bad at table tennis! I wonder if that Vulindlela Youth Club still exists?

I must touch briefly on when I attended Luveve Primary School and met one of my Grade 4 equivalent recently qualified teachers whose name was Stanley Kudeni Johnson Bhebhe. He was under my dad's tutelage, but regardless of that, he genuinely thought I was a good student and we got on quite well. His name was to come up again later in my life, as you will read on....So it came to pass, one mid-year, my parents relocated to Zvishavane (Shabanie) asbestos mining town, and there I was to spend a year and a half of the remainder of my primary education, at Gresham Government School, and for all my sins, the only time I studied Shona formally, and as I recall, dismally flunked it! Luckily, it wasn't a compulsory qualification for my secondary school, which saw me going back to my place of birth where dad had first taught, uMzingwane (Matebeleland) to join my brother who was now back there for boarding school.

The four years spent there deserve a whole dedicated book of their own, if one is to do that period justice. But because I need to fast forward to Zimbabwe's independence, I shall only highlight the odd anecdote.

That table tennis I was telling you about saw the late NUST Professor Lindela Ndhlovu and I, thrashing it out between us as alternate reigning school table tennis champions (ping-pong) for several years. He was very good at it, and he was also seriously adept at Science and Mathematics! I wasn't surprised therefore when in later life, he was top man at NUST.

Those were also the guerilla war years, when various distinguished/prominent speakers would be invited by the Students Union to the school to ostensibly give us inspirational theology speeches and others (e.g., Bishop Abel Muzorewa), only for them to clandestinely kindle the revolutionary spirit in the students, as they delved into human injustices, politics and oppression, unbeknown to the white School Principal and other authorities.

This conscientized and inspired the older ones amongst us, or those who were close enough to guerilla recruiters, to abscond school altogether during the school holidays, never to return until 1979/80 at the end of the war. Because of where we were, i.e., Matebeleland, many crossed into Zambia to join ZAPU, while others from Mashonaland (during school holidays) absconded into Mozambique to join ZANU. I couldn't possibly name all of them, but brother to a school friend David, was among the most prominent ones to do so, and both David and I were never surprised because he'd always been very vocal and passionate about politics at school. He's ex- Ambassador Agrippa Mutambara. Great guy who looked after me then like his own brother.

My music passion continued unabated, aided by me convincing my dad to get me that hitherto portable radio I mentioned. In between studies, I religiously followed and entered many radio competitions hosted by Zim legendary broadcasters Webster Shamu, Ephraim Chamba, Patrick Bajilla, Ishmael Kadungure, Wellington Mbofana, and many others, as well as winning a host of prizes for pop chart prediction competitions on international stations like LM Radio to boot! My school pals marvelled at how I could pull off serious grades, whilst multitasking with music!

My love of cars would see me and my "club" of friends going at weekends, to sit by the Beit Bridge Bulawayo-Gwanda Road, to spot different exotic makes of cars travelling from South Africa, and that really fuelled my already budding enthusiasm for automobiles, which is my second passion after music, to this day. Those that know me will confirm that I'm a dyed in the wool petrolhead, so to speak. I daydreamed and promised myself that I'd one day go overseas to indulge my passion in both music and cars, because I'd also read a lot about motor shows like The Geneva Motor Show, in various periodicals, and in fact started collecting books and scrapbook cut outs on cars, planes and trains! Some of our senior college friends who'd left had gone overseas for further study by then, and from anecdotes and letters to their friends and family, the seed to live overseas was firmly planted.

But there was to be the little matter of a 20-year long detour or so, when I joined the Rhodesia Broadcasting Corporation (renamed ZBC), while I was still awaiting finalisation of my paperwork to come to college England.

So, from my secondary days, I did not just acquire academic qualifications, but practical skills like farming also. I was Vice Chairman of the Young Farmer's Club (as well as Photographic Club) by the time I left. We had a great tutor who ran it by the name of Mr. Kanengoni, who used to run all things agricultural at the college including orchard, grounds, and school farm, as I recall. Great inspirator. I also made a lot of friends, some of whom I would meet later in life...

While impatiently waiting to process my overseas paperwork after my secondary schooling, I applied and joined a 12-month Hotel Management apprenticeship course at Meikles Hotel in Harare, and my first stay was with Mr. James Manyika, who was headmaster at Chitsere Government Primary School in (National) Mbare. He was a family friend and colleague of my dad's. So, this was my first introduction to the Harare ghetto life, after the Bulawayo one. More about Mbare later...

At Meikles, coincidentally, I met an old school friend, Alvord Chatikobo, who was also on the course. So, I was glad that I was not alone in Harare. We were both to witness a phenomenon we had never known about until then, but which later helped us in years to come. One of our senior managers was a Mr. Glatz, very nice white American gentleman. He had lots of interesting anecdotes from around the world in his youth. He also had a serious affliction for suddenly shouting "Bombs! Bombs!", and he'd get totally disoriented for a couple of minutes and would scurry for cover. It was then explained to us by one of the white duty managers that Mr. Glatz was suffering from the effects of being bombed in the Vietnam War and this was a psychological condition that affected some ex-service personnel. So right there, was our raw introduction to Post Traumatic Stress Disorder (PTSD), and little did we know that we'd meet this phenomenon in 1979/80 with our own friends, siblings, workmates, and associates when they came back from the guerrilla war.

I could totally understand how some of them felt and acted, and were extremely nervous in certain dispositions, and this helped me greatly in understanding what they'd been through, and most importantly, how I could interact and help communicate and negotiate certain situations with them. I had an ex-combatant cousin, for instance, who thought playing military practical jokes with live ammunition was okay, and many family members didn't understand this. There was no debriefing or professional counselling that many of those ex-combatants I met had been privileged to or continuously provided. But I'll let others tell their stories more authoritatively.

Unfortunately, my immediate young brother never came back from the war, and I'm sure there are many of us Zimbabweans who do not choose to shout from the rooftops about our losses, or right to entitlement to anything. They remain the true martyrs of the struggle, regardless of which flag they might have fought the war of independence under...RIP Ushe, in an unmarked grave somewhere.

So, one day, my friend Alvord advised me that he'd failed a ZBC audition some weeks back because he couldn't speak three languages fluently. Although deadline was long past, he kept bugging me to phone and find out if the vacancy was still going. I relented after a few prompts and was promptly invited to come attend an audition.

Mr. Dominic Mandizha oversaw the auditions at Mbare Studios. He gave me a script or other to translate and voice in the 3 languages, and do a mock presentation of a pop programme etc. (Another BIG MISTAKE!)

Remember my Mpopoma days with dad making us listen to the news etc. and me mimicking the announcer? Well, of course I was in familiar territory here…This audition was a stroll in the park! Must pay tribute to 2 technical operators who helped here, Mukoma Gerry Mwandiambira and Mukoma Eric Mugwenhi!

Mr. Mandizha said to wait on the bench at Reception while he listened back to the output. He came to reception where I was barely 15 minutes later and said: "You've got the job. When can you start?" I went on a long explanation about how I was in the middle of a management course while waiting for my UK university papers to come through, and would need to give notice etc. etc., to which he simply replied: "John, I don't think you heard me…I said when can you start?"

Well, come the following Monday, yours truly was now behind the microphone. The rest is not "Geography" …I temporarily which subject it is! 🤔😛

And so, another important lesson in my life beckons. I must have been doing something right at the radio station because even though usually the preserve of more senior and experienced personnel, I was assigned a Breakfast Show in my first year. I think my recruiter (Dominic Mandizha), was immensely vindicated. Through nurturing by my senior broadcasters like Amon Nyamambi, Cyrus Ntini, Godwin Mbofana, Elias Gwata, Ben Mazonde, Brighton Matewere, Joseph Masuku, Jabulani Mangena and many others, I quickly mastered the craft! As if that wasn't enough, in my second year, I was put in charge of recruiting (auditioning) new announcer/producers, as the station was expanding. At the first session of these, who was to turn up? Lo and behold, if it wasn't our Stanley Bhebhe, my Grade 4 ex-teacher! We had a very good laugh and am glad to say my ex-teacher passed with flying colours, and I welcomed him aboard! What did that teach me about getting on with everyone you meet as much as possible?

My ex-teacher became my colleague, even though now junior, and I had to show him the ropes. Then an old school mate from Mzingwane boarding school days (a Vice School Captain during my time), also joined (Luke Mnkhandhla). I bet he's glad for never confiscating my portable school radio when I might have been a bit over enthusiastic about listening schedules way back at college!

These two became some of my closest allies at Radio 2. Things could have turned out very differently had I not got on with my ex-school mates and teacher in this case. (For the shoe was now firmly on the other foot, so to speak)!

My radio days between 1973 – and 1980, deserve a dedicated book on broadcasting. It would not be doing justice to them to just rush through them.

Suffice to say after 2 years, I moved to a Commercial Production House, right up until 1981, when we were recruited by Mukoma Webster Shamu to found Radio 3. The history of that station deserves a whole book on its own. Suffice to say my fingerprints were embarrassingly all over its conception and roots, and I was heading it by the time I bailed out for pastures new...overseas, in 1991. I just felt I'd outgrown my pond, so to speak. No big deal...besides had always hankered after overseas sojourn. In fact, Big Sam (Mike Mhundwa) and yours truly, are the only remaining surviving founder members, as of 2023. And as I'm not given to making grand claims, I'll one day return to that story in detail...if we're spared.

I must also mention here that one of my ex-colleagues who joined our Blackberry Productions after me (late Ray Chirisa), and I, made broadcasting history when at the commercial production house, by being first to extend Radio 2's broadcasting hours (which usually ended Friday's shortly after 2200hrs), to midnight, when we launched a music show called The Black Label Happening! (This was before Radio 3, in terms of chronology. A precursor of pop radio, in retrospect!)

So, what were our interactions with others more privileged than our ethnic group, as the war ravaged, and independence beckoned?

We did not rest on our laurels as far as career and business development. While we toiled and struggled to both support our families, and clandestinely contributed materially to the war effort, some of us lucky ones rose through the management hierarchies of where we were. Our European counterparts, in my circumstances, did not wish to wait for the war to change things. They are pro-acted. Late broadcasting legend Ephraim Chamba and I were appointed first black directors of our larger amalgamated Production Houses, and I also decided to pursue business studies part time at the UZ. (I was to return to UZ on a part time basis again years later).

My other passion of cars saw me rub shoulders and socialise with many racial types who were into cars. Chiefly I remember one of my trusted garages was motor rallying legend's Reg Lombard, and I would spend lots of time chatting motoring, modifications, rallying etc. each time I was at his garage. I was also to host the World of Sport TV programme for a while much later, besides my TV musical and game shows after independence, and this also took me to Donnybrook Racing Track many a time, besides meeting all other sporting persons from both sides of the racial divide.

A fellow resident and friend from Kambuzuma, and myself, (also fellow contributor to this book, Township Boys), also became possibly the first young guys to own Mercedes vehicles in Harare before 1980. To put that in perspective, they usually were the preserve of the very affluent Europeans or black businesspeople. It felt good for me to get one using my own money, never mind very young age too. Mercedes cars were not for people on their way up, but rather those who'd already arrived!

Again, it was through the power of good relations and associations with those that I did business with, because as far as mine was concerned, I got that at a very fair price because of said cordial relations.

Hosting various commercial/sponsored programs then mostly in the hands of non-indigenous blacks, also taught me how to interface with the "white" corporate world, as well as thriving Asian community, most of whom remain dear to me to this day. Within those circles I was also to meet blacks who were on the way up or already there. Luminaries like Enos Chiwura from the breweries, the late Mukoma Etherton Mpisaunga from Lintas Advertising, Mukoma Paul Mkondo and Steve Chigorimbo from Southampton Insurance company, and Mukoma Elias Madzimure from Prudential Insurance Company, to name a few. In fact, I got a lot of inspiration from working and co-presenting Money and Life (Mari NeHupenyu Hwevanhu), with Mukoma Paul. He taught me lifelong lessons about money, wealth creation, humility, and just downright niceness to all those you meet. There are many others that I may revisit one day in a more appropriate forum. So came the years/period of integration, for it was a process not an event. In Harare, I'm proud to have lived in various typical "townships": Mbare, Kambuzuma, Marimba Park, Highfield Houses and Beatrice Cottages, before slowly moving into the slightly gentrified suburbs (Marimba Park, Braeside, Arcadia, Ardebennie and Southerton). My pal and colleague Mike Mhundwa and I were quite possibly some of the first blacks to move into the first northern suburb of Greystone Park, Harare.

We were very few blacks then, but I must applaud the few white property landlords who were colour blind. This was before I eventually bought my own house in the same area.

This integration was a learning curve for both sides of the racial divide because it was shocking enough for my neighbours to have people of colour living in their neighbourhood and shopping in their precincts, who were not domestic helpers. Some were incredulous, others took it on the chin, and plenty more as independence beckoned, accepted it in resignation. I cannot say I ever met any distinct hostility, but you could read the surprise in their eyes, downright discomfort in others, and stark bewilderment in a few, as we started patronising restaurants, nightclubs, and other night spots, town centres and cinema houses.

Generally, though, I'd like to think those that came across some of us, learnt a very precious and surprising lesson that we were essentially all the same, and the stereotype and hype they had been brought up on was not justified. Let's face it, we'd all been brought up on a diet of segregation, and to now share backyards and amenities was a cultural shock to both.

The depth of ignorance/unease if we can call it that, of mixed races living together wasn't starker than what happened when I started playing reggae music performed by white groups on Radio (Paul Simon's Mother and Child Reunion, Rolling Stones' Cherry Oh Babe, Eric Clapton's I Shot the Sheriff, UB40 and others). In fact, there was a white reggae group I played on air variously the first time but didn't have any videos for me to air on my TV show, such that a white listener drove up to the studios at Pocket's Hill after my show, just to verify these guys were white from the album sleeve! (There was no animal called the Internet then children!)

My experiences may not be universal, but we can only speak as we find. Largely, it was a smooth transition for me, possibly because I always believed in treating people as I find them, and in my belief: A stranger is just a friend you haven't met. That belief seems to have served me well to this day.

Maybe, because of higher-than-average exposure on radio, and over exposure on TV, I was a bit of a known/familiar quantity to those same 'strangers' already, and it must have made shut doors easier for me to open, with everyone across racial lines. I found I always struck common ground with whomever I would run into, and they in turn would share company, trade jokes, hopes, fears and so forth. Very humbling.

If truth be told, some of my best buddies were the so-called common man in the street, the gardener, the office cleaner, and other humble professions. I learned a lot about people's lives and aspirations from doing live shows in remote parts of Zimbabwe, from mines to farm compounds, and hosting shows in more affluent surroundings with my old pal and co-presenter Allan Riddell (now sadly late). What a talent he was!

I also learnt posture and poise, public speaking, and presentation from reading TV news with Mervyn Hamilton. Though much senior than I in years, we shared a passion in cars, especially VW Golfs.

And so came about the 1980 Independence Celebration at Rufaro Stadium in Harare, with Bob Marley and the Wailers. That was arguably one of the highlights of my career. Hosting various radio and TV shows already, I was drafted in to present that musical concert. More rewarding however was the time we spent socialising with Bob Marley and his group, from the time they arrived in Zimbabwe until they left. My friend Mike Mhundwa, through various connections, acted as their chaperone throughout their visit, and I distinctly recall playing social soccer with Bob and his band mates, and just thoroughly enjoying ourselves. There were no airs or graces, just downright ordinary folk, though indeed much larger than life when on stage. I recall I used to chat a lot with late Tyrone Downie (keyboardist), who was extremely humble and likeable, when Bob was busy with the press and fans.

We shared and traded our hopes and aspirations for the new Zimbabwe and enjoyed long conversations and wise counsel from Bob Marley for hours on end. I remember asking him why he'd sung "Zimbabwe", and he said the lyrics pretty much spoke what he had on his mind. I asked if Jamaica was sorted politically, and about three hours later, we were still discussing "3rd World" politics.

So, the concert itself represented a lot of hope and goodwill for the newly born nation. There was trepidation in some, hope in others, elements of fear of the unknown that was evident on both sides of those who'd come back from the war, and those that had stayed behind. We were now in a melting pot that needed cool heads, goodwill, trust, brother/sisterhood, and holding each other's hands through the trying times that would inevitably follow.

As life would have it, there comes a stage in life when one feels the time has come to flee the nest. For me, various restless push/pull factors were at play, but it was only a question of time before I decided that the little detour I'd taken post-secondary school, to go overseas and study, should now end. I felt I'd outgrown my pond, basically.

Independent Zim came, with many promises and opportunities for some, while others got disillusioned along the way. The new could not sit comfortably with the old in some situations, especially when one may have felt the progress that we hoped to make as a nation, was slowly getting derailed. Others, and these include family members and friends who'd relocated back to Zimbabwe at independence, started retracing their steps to the diaspora. I was not immune to some of these compelling issues, and unfortunately sometimes at great cost to personal relationships, business endeavours and professional trajectories, but then life is a journey. One can never get to neither reach, nor write the last chapter of their life if they keep rereading the last one. And so, some ten years or so after independence, it was time to board that plane and say hello world...

If we are spared, one day I would like to contribute my perspective on life in the diaspora, as coincidentally for me, more than half my adult life has been spent abroad. There are stories to be told and lessons to be imparted for progeny.

Does one ever forget about their home country though? Not me! I might have been back to Zim only like three times or so in 30 years, but it is a country that remains dear to my heart, what with other family members still there. Zim also made me the person I am, and those hustling skills in Mpopoma to Mbare, helped me build a very strong constitution, especially as my first flat in the UK was in South London in Peckham, and Brixton was my hood. You just don't get more ghetto than that! Big up maan!

And then came a surreal moment around 1995 just outside Bounds Green Tube Station in North London, during a Tube train strike. From the traffic lights, in the company of my then Zambian born girlfriend, who did I spot, waiting for a minicab close to the tube station, waving his trademark white handkerchief, if not ex-Zambian President Dr Kenneth Kaunda himself, stuck trying to get to a meeting at Hotel Intercontinental somewhere in the West End of London, as I was to find out after self-introduction. I offered to take him there in my squashed 2 + 2 Nissan ZX Coupe sports car! His aide (whom we had to drop off somewhere along the way) and my girlfriend, squashed at the back, and the President and I enjoyed the more spacious front seats!

A lot of private and personal memories and memoirs were traded in that 90 minute or so drive, in English I could understand, and ChiChewa with my girlfriend between them! Dr Kaunda had a repository of wisdom to pass to future generations. (He'd left office by then). I distinctly remember reminiscing about his old friend Robert Mugabe, Dr Hastings Banda, the Federation, the armed struggle, the bombings they suffered at the hands of the South African Army because they hosted Zi guerilla camps...and all the surrounding challenges that took us to where Zimbabwe was then.

He was a strong advocate of wishing the old/experienced leaders to be co-opted into the mix of current government leaders, so they could be part of an advisory council, to help incumbents navigate statecraft, rather than perceive them as enemies and confine them to the dustbins of history, and in the process, lose years of invaluable expertise and experience.

I have never been more humbled.

He was down to earth, no airs no graces, and how many people can claim to have been recounted the Zambian perspective of Zimbabwe's guerilla war from the horse's mouth? Privately?

Dr Kaunda sadly passed before I took him up on that warm invitation to Lusaka!

Where you led, we sure will all follow. I personally look forward to your wise counsel when we do meet next, in the afterlife…a world without end.

Life…

I dreamt a dream and lived a dream.

My life has not been such a bad gig after all, all told. So…Thank you God for everything I didn't deserve…

Peace…

John-the-Boss

(John Matinde).

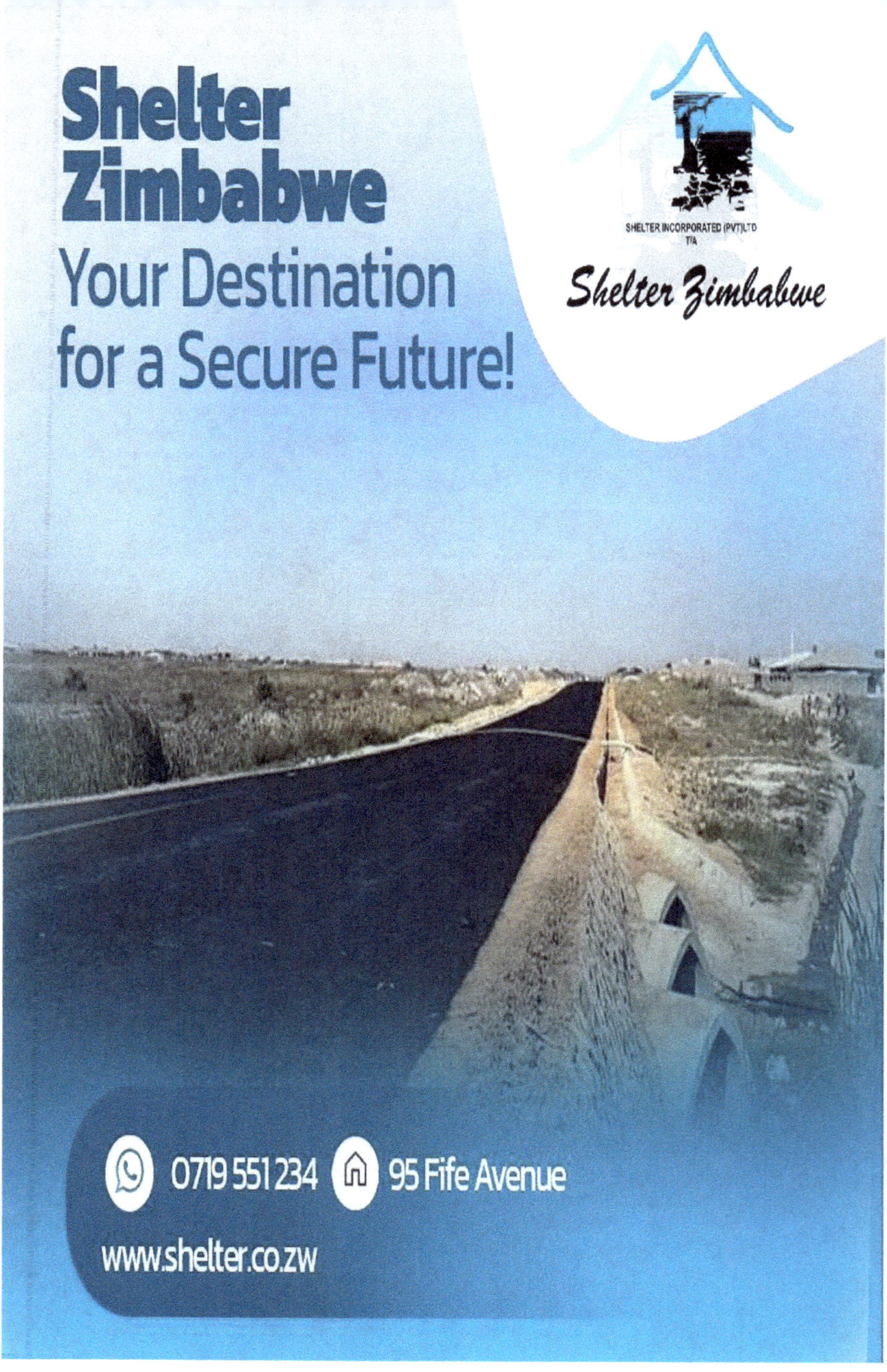

Shelter Zimbabwe
Your Destination for a Secure Future!

Shelter Zimbabwe

0719 551 234   95 Fife Avenue
www.shelter.co.zw

Chapter Nine: Ghetto Short Stories
By Richard Tanyanyiwa

WEEKEND, GHETTO STYLE!

Now that I am back in near full lockdown, I might as well ramble to keep myself going. I know there are many negative events taking place worldwide at this point in time and so I have elected to look at the lighter side of life just to provide a relief from the deluge of news that brings out the darker side of humanity.

So what is this so called "Lighter Look" that I am promising you? Tales from my childhood are a favourite. Today I would like to focus on weekends during my childhood. These were celebrated like holidays and I remember the weekend sights and sounds from my childhood ghetto of Mbare in the heart of the Capital, Harare. In fact the Capital got the name "Harare" from our good old "Mbare". The Capital used to have a colonial name (Salisbury) and our ghetto was called Harare. Soon after Independence this was changed and our ghetto took on its current name, Mbare.

Every Friday, all schools and most businesses wound down at lunch time (usually One o'clock afternoon) and in places like Mbare it was the onset of "ShowTime". The early signs of weekend cheer began when you left the school gate heading homeward to be greeted by the sound of music blaring from almost every household that had a stereo system, playing the latest sounds from the likes of The Hurricanes, Jimi Hendricks, Grand funk Railroad, Deep Purple (Heavy rock music used to rule the roost!) , The Jacksons and other local and international artists too numerous to mention, depending largely on who was topping the music charts of the those early seventies.

The stereos of the day had detachable speakers and it was the in-thing to bring these outside of the house and play music full blast to whoever was passing by! This had a dual effect of showing off who had the latest sound system as well as who possessed the latest, chart-topping music! Points were awarded for those who could play the latest music at the loudest volume and manage to drown out competing neighbors! I don't know how it never bothered us to have one household playing one heavy rock band full blast while the next door neighbor was playing a different band also full blast! Sometimes the effect was enough to tear off one's eardrums but somehow ours held on as this never bothered us. In fact we loved it and happily took part in this signature ghetto weekend entertainment ritual! By the way, our houses were closely hunched together (semi-detached) but guess what? No one ever complained! We somehow took this all in stride as it was all part of ushering in the weekend! We could not imagine a weekend without these sounds dominating the weekend landscape.

Once we got home and changed from school uniform to "home " clothes it was time to go out into the streets and take in the weekend mood. One of the greatest spectacles was the stream of workers coming in from the adjacent industries. They used to form a long line that resembled a parade. Youngsters of my age would stand by to admire this parade which presented an awesome display of the latest fashion trends. You would witness high heels so high that you wondered how these guys could maintain balance wearing them, but somehow they did!

Bell bottomed, bright colored trousers and floral shirts were not uncommon among this lot. I will not forget fashion outfits of the day such as safari suits, jeans, high waist trousers and midi skirts and high heeled sandals among the women. Sunglasses were also a regular fashion statement of the day. When the industrial parade had made its way into the ghetto, it was time to visit the local shops to see who was buying the most groceries for family. Delivery bicycles doing door to door deliveries could be seen crisscrossing the whole neighborhood. The more imaginative people used wheelbarrows to carry their groceries which usually included foodstuffs and popular fizzy drinks like Coca-Cola, Fanta, Pepsi and others.

The other hotbeds of activity were, of course, the shebeens and official liquor outlets which had roaring business; selling takeaways during the daytime and then hosted late night revelers later on. Just as the sun was setting, a new type of parade took over. Smartly dressed ladies donning fancy wares like wigs, miniskirts, stiletto shoes, lipstick and other make up could be seen taking over the streets as they were made their way to the shebeens, bars and night clubs. At this stage most would be unaccompanied but this situation changed when they got to their targeted destinations. If you were still able to stay out on the streets long enough you would be able to witness the reverse parade when the official outlets closed and most would emerge in the company of "clients". Our parents protected us from witnessing such later views by imposing a sunset curfew on us. You could only witness this by sneaking out at night when the parents went to sleep. The cacophony of competing music went well into the night and sometimes into daylight for those into hard partying! I don't know how we could stomach these competing sounds, but I don't recall anyone ever complaining. This was all part of ghetto life and for us it was take it or leave it. In fact we actually loved it!

The whole events of Friday night were wild enough but come Saturday and you were treated to an early calm before the storm when the ghetto erupted again into Saturday partying which went on into early Sunday morning! Such was the mood of the weekend that you looked forward to it with eagerness as it provided us with our weekly dose of entertainment and parties. Also, on Saturdays, most kids like myself were given pocket money by our parents that enabled us to watch afternoon movies (James Bond, Bruce Lee and Western movies mostly) at the famous Stoddard Hall. Cartoons like Mickey Mouse and Tom and Jerry were a big hit with our ages!

These events, Resembling latter day street parties and fashion parades constituted the highlight of the weekend 'especially the free music parties out on the streets. Come Sunday and we would go to church and then proceed to Rufaro Stadium, usually to watch our ghetto favourite home team, Dynamos *DeMbare* playing a rival team. The outcome of such games would make topics for debate and argument for the entire week to come. By the time Sunday evenings came you could feel an eerie silence descend upon the tired ghetto as preparations began for the week ahead. Some of us would suddenly remember that there was homework to be done and quickly got busy to avoid a Monday morning date with the teacher's stick when same was called in before classes began.

Monday to Thursday was rather quiet but come Friday, the ghetto would religiously explode into its usual weekend mode with renewed vigor! Did we ever get bored or tired of this? No ways! Such was the unique pulse and heartbeat of ghetto life that it can never be matched elsewhere and I am so proud to have had a ringside seat to this spectacular weekend show. It's a pity that this weekend party mood of the ghetto has now been lost and somehow no one seems to be able to bring back those beautiful good old days! Dzangove ndangariro! (Only fond memories remain!) Happy Friday!

THE LEGEND OF MHAKRING: MBARE'S SCHOOLYARD SCOURGE

Let's not sugarcoat this: Mbare, back in the pre-independence days, was no playground. It was the original "Hunger Games," and right in the middle of it stalked a wiry demon-child by the name of Mhakring—sometimes called Mhaka, sometimes Maikoro, depending on how fast your teeth were chattering. Imagine a scrawny kid, ribs counting themselves out like xylophone keys, eyes glowing with mischief, and a broken fan belt swinging from his waist like Batman's utility belt. Except, Batman saved people. Mhakring? He taxed them.

This pint-sized warlord wasn't just a boy—he was a cautionary tale in Bata Toughies. Mothers would whisper his name like a bedtime horror story: "Sleep now, or Mhakring will find you." And we believed it. Forget Spider-Man or Joker. Mhakring was our Thanos—minus the purple skin, but with the exact same ambition to make half the school population cry before breakfast.

His kingdom? A choke point near his house. That was his customs office, his Beitbridge border post. Once you hit that path, you had three options:
1. Pay the toll (pocket money, lunch, or whatever valuables you had).
2. Catch the Ndare Special—his slide tackle so ferocious it should've had its own FIFA referee.
3. Take the detour—a back-breaking hike that felt longer than Moses' 40 years in the wilderness.

We used to say: "Cross Mhakring's road without paying? That's like swimming across Kariba with a raw steak tied to your back—you're not making it out alive."

And that fan belt… my friend, that wasn't just rubber. That was Excalibur forged in the fires of Mbare industry. He wore it like John Cena with a WWE belt. One lash, and your lunch box opened itself in fear.

But make no mistake: Mhakring wasn't some clueless thug. No, this was a strategic mastermind, a streetwise Robin Hood—if Robin Hood had decided, "You know what, I'm keeping the loot for myself and my dropout squad." His favorite targets?

The Beatrice Cottages fat cats. You know the type: kids who packed lunches like mini-Hotel Intercontinentals, their Tupperwares overflowing with Vienna sausages, samosas, cheese sandwiches—while the rest of us were chewing on plain maputi. Mhakring would let the broke kids pass like a benevolent dictator, then pounce on the rich ones like a hyena at a braai. Those luxury lunch boxes? Straight into his plastic bag, redistributed among his goons like United Nations aid parcels.

His cruelty hit absolute peak levels on prize-giving days. Picture this: you've worked your guts out all term, dreaming of that book prize. The moment you step outside the school gates, boom—there's Mhakring, crouched like a troll under a bridge. "Nice book. It would be a shame if someone… shredded it." Certificates got turned into instant confetti, unless you bribed him with snacks. Kids started smuggling their prizes home like illegal goods—hidden in jerseys, wrapped in brown paper, or entrusted to a cousin built like Mike Tyson.

And God help you if you rocked up in a fresh uniform. New khakis? Brand-new blazer? Mhakring would demand a "commission," or else force you to roll in the dust like a pig auditioning for a Sadza commercial. Parents used to send their kids to school looking like scruffy soldiers—not because they were poor, but because looking sharp was basically an invitation to war.

The fear was so deep that kids would beg parents for "toll money" before school. Imagine that: your mom giving you five cents for maheu and another ten cents "just in case Mhakring is hungry today." Snitching to teachers? Out of the question. Mhakring's revenge threats sounded like deleted scenes from a horror movie.

But every king has his enemies. Mhakring's only weakness? The big brothers. High school boys who acted like vigilantes, avenging their younger siblings. When they caught him, they served justice Mbare-style: quick, loud, and educational. He'd disappear for weeks, limping around like a retired war vet, but then—like a bad Nollywood sequel—Mhakring always returned, eyes full of vengeance, fan belt polished and ready.

Then one day, just like that, the reign ended. His father retired and carted the whole family off to the rural areas. My guy was exiled like Napoleon, shipped out to a land where the only victims were chickens and goats. The relief in Mbare? You could feel it in the air. Parents stopped budgeting for bribes, kids walked to school singing freedom songs, and prize-giving days finally looked like actual celebrations instead of hostage negotiations.

Still, legends never die. For years after, his name was recycled by parents as a disciplinary tool: "Bath, or I'm calling Mhakring." And trust me, when you've lived under his rule, you don't test that kind of threat. Even now, decades later, his name makes grown men shiver, laugh, and instinctively check if their pockets are empty.

So here we are, post-COVID, dredging up the memory of a skinny tyrant with a dream, a fan belt, and unmatched slide tackle technique. Mhakring—you menace, you strategist, you legend. Wherever you are now, I pray you're taxing goats instead of traumatizing school kids.

Long live the legend of Mhakring—the only kid who ever turned National into a one-man toll plaza!

HOW SWEET! (With Extra Zing)

Growing up in Mbare was no fairy tale—unless your version of a fairy tale includes chronic power cuts, mystery meat, and the occasional uninvited relative showing up like a boss-level villain. If life had roses, we only saw thorns. But somehow, out of all that dust and drama, I walked away with some of the best memories... and a lifelong trust issue with door knocks.

Month-end was our holy grail. That's when Dad, the family's one-man economic engine, got paid. And for about 72 glorious hours, we lived like royalty—chicken royalty. That was when beef, chicken, or fish made a brief cameo on our plates before vanishing for another 27 days, replaced by the usual suspects: kapenta, beans, cabbage, and offal so chewy they doubled as dental training.

Now picture this: it's chicken day. I've been dreaming about drumsticks all week. I can smell the stew from the gate. My stomach is composing a thank-you speech. Then... knock knock. I open the door, and boom—instant heartbreak.

Standing there like a horror movie jump scare: my uncle, his wife, and a squad of human appetites staring back at me. I swear I saw a chicken leg vanish into thin air. My old man sealed the betrayal by tossing my brother a coin and saying, "Go buy lacto for the kids." Translation: chicken is for the visitors. I felt that one in my soul.

I swore revenge that day—not just for me, but for every child who's ever watched their dream meal rerouted by a surprise relative.

And then, a master plan hatched. Literally.

Next chicken day, I launched Operation Block-a-Visitor. I positioned myself like a bouncer outside the gate right after school. The mission: intercept any incoming threats before they breached the premises. Sure enough, just as the sun dipped and the smell of gravy began to flirt with the air, I saw them—a convoy of relatives approaching with purpose. I blocked the gate like a seasoned security guard and hit them with:

"Who are you looking for?"

"The teacher's house," they said.

Bingo.

"Well," I replied solemnly, "he transferred. New address' in town. Want directions?"

They nodded. I gave them an expertly vague route that guaranteed at least two hours of wandering and internal family arguments. Off they went.

Back inside, it was high-fives and hero worship. That chicken meal hit different—victory-flavored. Even my usually stingy older brother offered me an extra wing in gratitude. I was a legend.

Until karma knocked. Literally.

About an hour later, the same train of chicken bandits returned—sweaty, dusty, and very unchicken-fed. Apparently, one of them had ratted me out, telling Dad about "some mischievous little boy who misled them."

Cue the parental roll call. Dad lined up me and my brothers like suspects on a game show: Who Wants to Avoid a Beating? Lucky for me, our parents had spaced us barely a year apart. We looked like a factory batch of troublemakers. No one could identify the exact culprit. I tried not to laugh. Something escaped anyway—I won't say from where, but it wasn't from my mouth.

So, did I pay for my crime? Technically no. Did I learn my lesson? Also no. But that chicken tasted like justice. And let's just say, next month, I was already planning phase two.

How sweet indeed!

COMMUTER OMNIBUS: KING OR VILLAIN?

This time there are no seat belts to fasten. Your best bet is to hold on to your seat, close your eyes and pray. This is one hell of a ride and be prepared to go to hell and back on this ride. The driver is a kamikaze pilot and will break every rule of the road with impunity. Not even the police can stop him on his day and when they do he can always take the "easy" way out. Welcome aboard a commuter omnibus and if you come out alive or in one piece then heaven help you!

Love them or hate them commuter omnibuses are the "stars" of the rush hour traffic. These guys rule the roost and can rewrite the driving manual any day, if not every day. These are the guys who have perfected the art of beating the morning traffic jams. You might be tempted to clap hands for them until you discover that they are responsible for creating the traffic jams in the first place. They drive on the wrong side of the road and in the face of oncoming traffic with a straight face, and if you don't give them way then prepare for an accident because these guys don't concede right of way easily, if at all. To go on a ride on the commuter omnibus is to test your guts to the limit. Be prepared to see the rule-book torn to shreds and be re-written all in the space of a short trip to town.

There are two ways to experience commuter omnibuses. You can either do so as a passenger in which case you hand over your life to them for the entire ride and pray that you arrive in one living piece or interact with them as a fellow motorist and be prepared to be bullied into giving them way whenever they sound their hooters and not only request permission for you to move over and allow them passage but sometimes actually proceed to perform some death-defying maneuver right in front of you well before you can consider their request! The question that begs is why ask for permission when you can act before that permission is granted. Was the "request" ever necessary in the first place?

Passengers are the biggest customers as well as the biggest victims of commuter omnibuses and their crews. To ride on one is to experience almost all of them and chances are that you will come out of the journey with a testimony on bad driving, poor treatment of passengers and foul language. These guys have mutated into a new breed of person who knows no respect for passengers young or old. They will unleash an outburst of foul language that will leave you dumbfounded in the presence of young and old, parent or child all with a straight face. I believe most regular passengers have devised a way of coping with all this behaviour which deserves a medal of honour.

Commuter omnibuses can break every rule of the road and I can never imagine a trip on one where the rulebook is not taken to pieces. It is almost as if the drivers will die of boredom if they stick to the rules. I am almost tempted to think that it is considered a disgrace to drive normally in their "code of misconduct". Believe me these guys have found their own admirers among their passengers only because they somehow get the job done when it comes to beating traffic jams. Who would not beat the jam if they are allowed to drive on any side of the road, ride over roadside kerbs and make u-turns in front of oncoming traffic or at the sight of a police roadblock! If you are "lucky" be prepared for a high speed chase with police hot on your tail. The commuter driver normally wins because he is a suicide bomber ready to take any risk that will help him escape from police.

All you have to pray for is that you get to your destination somehow and, God willing, in one piece. Commuter omnibuses literally monopolize the road accident statistics and I am tempted to think that they get embarrassed and feel let down when they hear of a traffic accident not involving one of their own.

Commuters omnibuses are almost a marvel to watch as they go about their daily business because one is guaranteed some form of action either in the form of some breath-taking stunt to get their own way or some hell ride that takes you through the alleys and byways and, depending on circumstances, don't rule out doing so in reverse! These guys must have attended their own school of driving for they all seem to subscribe to the same code of bad ,audacious, life-threatening, kamikaze-style driving.

There are a few commuter omnibus drivers who observe normal driving procedures but these are so few that they are an endangered species. Sometimes I am tempted to think that they are almost an embarrassment to their colleagues. Otherwise how come they are so few and why are their numbers actually dwindling? Generally the rules of the game seem to be that you must break every rule of the road and be prepared to use foul language in front of anyone who cares to listen.

I do not know if commuter omnibuses get their business from people who use their services for lack of choice or because, in the event that you get to the destination alive, then it must be job done because they tend to get there faster than anyone who cares to observe the rules of the road. Love them or hate them commuters are here to stay and judging by the stunts they perform on our roads I am tempted to ,grudgingly and with a heavy heart, crown them "kings of the road" Good Day.

THOSE FUNNY LANES!

Yesterday I mentioned how a friend lost an eye to an unknown assailant who launched from an alley. Today I just feel I have to talk about such alleys and the role they played in my hometown of Mbare. The whole township was built around a sophisticated web of such alleys which used to run between rows of our closely spaced houses. We used to call them "Masendiraini" and I figure the term could have derived from "Central lanes" as they used to run between rows of houses or "Sanitary lanes" as they provided access to council workmen to repair our frequently broken toilets. These lanes were such an integral part of ghetto life that I would like to focus on the role they played in my upbringing.

The one major role they played was as a lover's lane where young lovers could meet away from the eyes of adults. For some strange reason there was an unwritten law that they were out of bounds to parents. You could get to your girlfriend's house through this back route and smuggle her out right under her parent's noses! The more daring ones could also sneak into the girl's bedrooms at night and sneak out via the same route.

Come nightfall and these lovers lanes played host to an entirely different species of characters. They now became home to prostitutes who used them to quickly serve their clients and this was particularly true of those located near famous beer halls of my day which went under such names as "Mahovhorosi", "Marengenya" and "Mapitikoti"! Along with prostitutes they also played host to muggers who either worked in cahoots with the prostitutes or operated on their own for easy pickings from people who had enjoyed the forbidden fruit and were making their way home or back to the waterhole. Passersby could be dragged into the nearest lane for a quick search away from the public eye!

The lanes provided an easy and elaborate escape route for criminals under pursuit from the police or from irate mobs when they got surprised on the job! For us youngsters they also provide an easy bypass from bullies who used to charge us "toll fees" for passing on the streets! At one point one famous such lane was rumoured to be a hangout of a ghost called "Mary" who used to mascarade as a prostitute and then disappear on a would be client after unleashing a thunderous clap and leaving her clothes in a smouldering heap. Most such clients would then lose their heads in shock, sometimes never to recover!

These lanes also played host to some types who thought it humorous to stone or catapult passers-by or vehicles just for the fun of it, especially on events like New Year's Eve. Such was life in the ghetto and vicious though it might have appeared I would not have traded it in for any other for within it were the building blocks that have brought about yours truly!

GOOD OLD DAYS IN MBARE

It is a beautiful, Africa Day morning (Memorial Day here in USA) and once again I find myself traveling down memory lane to the days of my childhood in Mbare, a ghetto in my home country, Zimbabwe.

I grew up in a country where racism was rife and impacted all facets of life such as where one could live, which schools you could attend, what shops you could buy from, what places you could drink beer at and so forth. In fact, there was a time when you had to be certified by the state to be allowed to purchase luxuries such as bottled beer and to be permitted to drink from selected outlets which were deemed elite in those days! Among the criteria used for such entitlement was one's standard of education. My father, being a teacher, was a proud recipient of one such certificate which gave him license to drink in "cocktail bars", a badge of honor allowed to a privileged few!

This selective access to liquor drinking places led to the mushrooming of illegal, house based drinking outlets called shebeens. In Mbare there were some famous shebeens which went by fancy names like Whitegate, Sixteen's(pamdhara sixteen), Dongo's, Big Vee's or Diamond's . Although these outlets were illegal and suffered occasional police raids, the regime largely looked the other way and allowed them to flourish! I am reliably informed that, although they are a fading culture, a few such places operate up to this day.

The story of my life growing up in Mbare is incomplete without mentioning goings on in these shebeens where the working guys and petty criminals would outdo each other to show fellow patrons that they had more money. Famous nicknames such as *Divha Dollar* and *Mark Madhora* were earned in these outlets. It was not uncommon in those days for one of these famous patrons to just rock up in one such place where revelers are drinking and declare that he was buying all the beer in the shebeen and proceed to order everyone out except friends and ladies! The rest of the guys had no choice but to leave and go find another place to drink at. This was especially common around Christmas time after working people had been paid their annual bonuses! Instead of taking such money home to spend with family, most such guys preferred to show off at shebeens with such theatrics!

In those days I clearly remember one guy who drove around in a convoy of two taxis, one carrying himself and his girlfriend and the other carrying his jacket! Occasionally he would pass through crowded places and toss out wads of banknotes through the taxi window. Some people would sustain injuries in the resulting stampede to grab some of those monies! Rumor has it that even after buying his own car, one of these guys continued to hire a taxi to drive behind him, carrying only his jacket! You can imagine the fanfare when the guy arrived at the shebeen and parked his car and then have his jacket brought to him by the taxi following behind!

Karma did eventually catch up with most of these guys and some of them crash-landed when they lost their jobs and had to return to a life of lack and poverty! Whenever I visit this land of my childhood it is not uncommon to meet such former heroes of my day, now wearing clothing that has seen better days, begging for coins to buy a cigarette or to buy the cheaper traditional brew! Of course, in their heydays, they wouldn't be seen dead drinking such! I have no problem indulging them because they will always occupy their place in my memory as heroes of my childhood!

Among the traits these show offers were famous for was designer clothing and the way they used to walk! These guys developed a way of walking that was a cross between walking and bouncing (you had to see this dance like walk)! It was a well-choreographed act and when they walked past, people would stop, stare and marvel at this way of walking! It was a work of art and, last time I tried to imitate this "step" in order to demonstrate to my bemused children, I almost fell over backwards! I pity that there were no video cameras in those days because I would have captured those marvels to show our children who think these are mere fairy tales.

I still marvel at the way this environment of general lack brought about most of the luminaries who now occupy the upper echelons of present day Zimbabwe society! For quite some time after independence and out of nostalgia, it was not unusual to see most of them drive from the posh suburbs to come and patronize these shebeens! I am convinced that for some of us, this ghetto lifestyle was somehow imbued with seeds of determination to succeed as witnessed by the who is who of people who grew up in good old Mbare.

Good Day!

Chapter Ten: From the Village to the City via War
By Masimba Charles Chiganze

My names are Charles Masimba, Karl Mandla, or Stalin Organ Masimbah, but in the villages, I was simply known as Uncle Charlie. The first guerrilla tactic I mastered is the 'Terrain and Terrain Features.' I am part of the Chihwa, Bonga, Sigauke Mutambara totem. Originally, our surname was Mabika. My great-grandfather was nicknamed Chiganze because he was very wealthy and boastful. He had a large herd of cattle, six aunts, six sisters, and six daughters - all extremely beautiful. He was the only son. Most of his daughters were married for a good bride price of not less than a dozen cows.

VILLAGE

I am a Sagittarian, born in December 1960 in Gandiya village near Mbiriri School, in Rukweza, Makoni District. The midwife was my grandfather's eldest wife, Mbuya VaGuma. I was oversized, which is why she nicknamed me Masimba. The village was a close-knit society. Both the kraal head Mr. Gandiya and his brother were married to our aunts. My grandfather, his other younger brother, a Bishop of a sect, had several wives each. Mr. Killion Chiganze ruled the village with an iron fist. Everything was communal and equally shared. A cow was slaughtered on every big occasion like weddings, funerals, and Christmas.

Edgar Tekere's father and Jonah Mudhara of AFM started their missionary work in our village. We adhered to very strict religious and cultural norms. All the children were to be baptized, marry, and have a wedding. When the groom went to work in the towns, his new wife was allocated a hut and a small garden. She was only allowed to visit her husband's workplace after the harvesting season. She could only attend either the Anglican or AFM church.

Within its ten-kilometer radius, many people who later excelled in various fields of academia, religion, politics, and business were raised. The list includes Gandiya, Tekere, Makoni, Chipunza, Bakara, Rwodzi Duri, Mataranyika, Chirinda, Gwasira, Mabika, Chiganze, Chimuka, Mbiriri, Mbodza, Nyagumbo, and many others.

In 1967 when I was 6, I started school; my mother remained in the village. My father was the headteacher at Epiphany Mission, the first site settled by the Pioneer Column's Bishop Knight Bruce's Anglican team before they moved a few kilometers away to the present day St Faith's Mission, and later to establish the town Rusape.

As the Headteacher, he doubled as the Parish Warden of St Faith's mission, Epiphany was the nearest station. We stayed, just the two of us. The school only enrolled students up to Standard 3. My elder brother Timothy and my other relatives who were in upper primary school were sent to boarding schools. When the land tenure came around the 1940s, the Anglican church divided its land, giving villagers small plots.

Most were descendants of the servants of early white settlers, who accompanied the Pioneer Column, along with a few locals, retired African priests, and deacons. The atmosphere was very conservative and reserved.

In late 1968, my father was transferred to Musaringo school, some 30 kilometers away in the Gandanzara area. It was a demotion but in fact, it was a blessing in disguise. Musaringo catered up to Standard 6. It was at the center of more than a dozen other schools, including Zuze, Gwasira, Haizoswi, Couge Kloof, Chinyama, Rugoyi, St Killion's, Chinono, St. Cosmas, Gananzara, Chikuruwo, Majakwara, St Maria, and nearby was a big business center and clinic.

Father Chitsike, who was both a priest and school manager, arranged for our transport with the local bus company. The arrangement was such that after leaving passengers in Rusape, they would drop the new replacement teacher with his goods at Epiphany, pick us up, then head to Rusape to pick regular passengers and drop us at Musaringo School. My father and I, along with all our household items, arrived at the new school around 3 in the afternoon. We were shown a newly built, large house - the biggest in the compound - as ours. Within a few minutes of the bus's arrival, more than 20 juvenile boys joined us, joyfully helping to unload and settle us in. When it was dusk they all left to their respective homes. Come time to cook, there was no firewood. At Epiphany, there were big eucalyptus trees planted by the missionaries and firewood wasn't a problem. At Musaringo, like any other communal rural area, it was heavily deforested. Luckily, there was one boy who lived nearby. My father asked him to go buy us a loaf of bread at the nearby shops. The following day we boarded the first bus out, going back to the village. During that holiday, my father bought a paraffin primer stove, and luckily one of his aunties was married nearby. He made prior arrangements for a cord of firewood.

When schools opened in 1969, it was a full house. Now it was my father, me, my elder brother Innocent, who used to stay with Mbuya, and my young sister Tambisa who was starting Grade one, and two other cousins from the Nyagumbo family. We were staying in the newest and biggest school house. Mother remained behind in the village. Brother Timothy continued at the boarding school.

Life was filled with activities and adventures. The population was larger. Sporting and other extracurricular activities were conducted with surrounding schools. Religion was diversified as most schools were of different church denominations. Some folks even held traditional functions, unlike at Epiphany which was strictly Anglican.

Father now didn't have to worry about sending his children and numerous dependents to boarding schools for upper primary schools. We were now being exposed to a wider world. Father joined the church Men's Fellowship Wabhuwi Guild. At that time, it was not yet common in Anglican Churches, so he spent most of his time with .At that time, it was not yet common in Anglican Churches, so he spent most of his time with Methodist members from nearby churches. They reciprocated; our house was always full of visitors. Soon, we had many real and imagined relatives, and especially on Sundays after church, it was always a full house with uncles, aunties, cousins, and church mates. It was an honor to be seen at the big house. They came with different gifts, and the older girls made sure that before they left, they completed all the menial chores, such as helping clean pots, fetching water, sweeping the yard, tending the garden, and washing and ironing.

My grade 6 and 7 teacher was very strict. His preferred method of discipline was a whip and various sorts of punishments. Luckily, my father was the sports master. My brother and I were included in all school trips. He gave us some personal academic coaching as he was a National Grade Seven examination marker.

SECONDARY SCHOOL

My brother, Innocent, enrolled for Form one at St Augustine's Mission, where our elder brother Timothy was. I passed my Grade seven examinations in 1973. Unlike my brothers, I went to St Faith's Mission for Secondary Education. It was an Anglican Church-run boys-only school. I was in the last batch to be taught by white missionary teachers. Discipline was very strict. Classes started at 6.30 am, then breakfast at 8. It was porridge, milk, and bread. After supper at 6, up to 8.30 was study time. Uniforms were khaki shorts and safari jackets, no jackets, jerseys, or coats, no matter the weather. Sunday church service was six to eight, then breakfast.

I was in Form 1R (Red or Rubbish), 1G (Green). The first to be enrolled were mostly boys from Salisbury. They sort of imagined themselves as more superior. Most of them were very delinquent, smoking, sneaking out on weekends to nearby villages for beer. They always had the latest fashion and music and plenty of pocket money. Most of us in 1R, like me, were sons of civil servants and peasant families.

There were three streams of Form 1 and 2s, then only one stream for Form 3 and 4 classes. This was the bottleneck education system. To proceed to form 3, some dropped out on their own due to financial problems, but screening was based on one's discipline and academic records. Out of 120 who enrolled for Form 1, only 36 proceeded to form 3. In 1976, I was accepted for form 3, my results were excellent: 6 As and 3 Cs. With an RJC certificate, someone could easily join the civil services, get a clerical job, or enroll in a vocational college. When in Form 3 or 4, one was automatically a senior and had some privileges. I became the 6th most powerful person. First was the Captain and his Vice, all in form 4, then the Designate Captain and his Vice, all from Form 3, then the Form 4 class monitor, then me, the Form 3 class monitor, then the timekeeper, Chief Church Server, Library Monitor, followed by 6 other prefects, from Form 3 and Form 4 .Prefects sat at the high table in the dining hall and stayed in small cabins, either in pairs or groups of three, while the rest of the students were housed in hostels accommodating between ten and thirty pupils each.

MOBILIZATION

PaMadetere, St Faiths is where it all started. By 1972, the war had started in the Northern part of Zimbabwe, especially the Mt Darwin area. In our class were two guys from there. They talked about their experiences and first-hand encounters with guerrillas. There were also newspaper stories and Rhodesian propaganda leaflets. In form 2, we studied the French Revolution and in Form 3, Contemporary European History, the 1st and 2nd World Wars, and the Russian Revolution. I read a book, "Whispering Death" by Daniel Carney, which was filmed with James Bond about the Bush War in Rhodesia. The main actor was an albino freedom fighter. I shared the book with my close friend and we started discussing different types of warfare. The cabin I shared with fellow form 3 prefects Philip Dumba and Morris Muzvuzvu. All form 3 students, especially former Form 1Rs, were always welcome. As prefects, we were exempted from switching off lights at 21.00 hours. So, we talked all night. A few form 2 boys were allowed, especially if they had extra food to share. One such guy was Sydney Fararai. His father Bobby was a businessman in Honde Valley near the Eastern Border. By early 1976, he would tell stories of Frelimo soldiers and early Zanla exploits, some with much exaggeration.

During that 1st term, one Sunday, the priest, Father Borerwa failed to attend the weekly sermon. The next week he explained that he had gone to court; his son-in-law, prominent businessman Mr. Samuriwo had been arrested, something to do with Chitepo's Death. He said Chitepo was his classmate at St Augustine's Mission. At that time, this didn't make much sense to me. But a group of students who had attended a Young Christian Movements workshop in Salisbury came back singing a lot of political revolutionary songs.

During the 2nd term holidays, back in the village, the last week of the holiday, one evening I was sleeping with my brother Timothy, who was on vacation from the University. In the village, there was choir practice; we were preparing for my cousin sister's wedding. Innocent, (in the village he stayed with our grandmother) was the organizer.

Around 8 pm we heard Innocent's voice calling us from the window. We peeped and saw the nozzles of guns. We woke up and he said the comrades were here at last. We accompanied him with the 2 comrades to the Pungwe which was at my grandfather's main house. The whole village was there, a lot of singing, now not of wedding bells but revolutionary songs. Then the commissar introduced himself and his colleagues. Those from my perception who seemed to be the senior commanders included Comrades Dusty, Choice Sipo, Sachiweshe, a very tall guy, and the late national hero Tonderai Nyika.

The commander Dusty had chosen my uncle's mansion as his command post. When he learned that my brother was studying at the university, he invited us for a private meeting. He organized for a radiogram. He had a case full of musical records, the latest Simanjemanje and Rumba were among the things he brought from Tanzania. He also had an assortment of reading materials, including magazines and novels. A bottle of clear beer or whiskey was always served to him. After one or two drinks, he would start to dance to his music.

He often joked about how exciting war was, and gave us a few lectures on guerrilla warfare. The following day, it was time for me to go back to school and for Timothy to return to university. A bus had been hired to ferry the wedding party, so transport was easily accessible. Dusty and two other comrades also got on the bus, claiming they were going shopping in Rusape. About five kilometers from the village, in the white commercial farming area, there was a roadblock set up by the Rhodesian soldiers. Just 100 meters away, seeing the roadblock, the comrades disembarked. At the checkpoint, we showed our school passes and the bus was allowed to proceed. Four hundred meters further down the road, the comrades were waiting. As usual, Comrade Dusty was always high.

I arrived at school on Wednesday afternoon. This time, the situation was tenser. The war had earnestly commenced in the Eastern Districts, so most of us had a story to tell. Also, the 1976 Soweto Uprising was in full swing. That same week, Chairman Mao died. In the prefects' cabin, we had long discussions about the war. We read magazines highlighting pictures and stories about Polisario PLO guerrillas, Samora Machel, Fidel Castro, Steve Biko, and the Soweto Uprising.

We decided the way forward was to cross over and join the Revolution. This was the jargon used then. The meeting was attended by Morris Muzvuzvu, Henry Mutasa, Philip Mbengeranwa, Cuthbert Marindire, Philip Dumba, myself, and others from Form 3 and Form 2. We didn't trust the Form 4s. Muzvuzvu and Farirayi were co-chairing as they had been exposed more to the war situation. Muzvuzvu came from Mutambara. We weighed all options, using either the Imbeza Forest route in Penhalonga or the Cashel Valley in Mutambara. We decided to split into two small groups. Muzvuzvu was to lead the Form 3s via Mutambara and Farirai the Form 2s via Penhalonga. The starting time was set for Sunday at 5 am.

On Sunday at 4 am, Muzvuzvu and I began waking up others in different dormitories. In the first round, everything was okay. Mutasa, however, could not be found; he had gone to visit his aunt in the nearby villages. Mbengeranwa woke up, washed his face, visited the toilet, and sat on his bed, but he didn't have the agreed kit or attire. He then confessed that he hadn't made up his mind.

And so, off we went, just the four of us. We walked 13 kilometers to Rusape town, hitchhiked to Mutare, and then again to Melsetter Junction. We then walked 5 kilometres to Mutambara Mission. Back at St Faith's, the other group that had proceeded through Penhalonga, met them two weeks later in Mozambique.

The next day at school, Mr. Chikodzore, the newly appointed first black Headmaster, sensed something amiss during his morning address. At the assembly, it was announced that Dumba had been demoted from being a prefect, Muzvzvu from being the timekeeper, and Chiganze from being the form 3 class monitor. Because most of the students knew what had taken place, they laughed at him. He then reported to the authorities. Mbengeranwa, who changed his mind at the last minute, suffered heavily. He was tortured by the Rhodesian Forces, who asked him where his friends had gone and who had funded them.

Of the whole group, only my cousin, Clifford Rwodzi, was killed during the Chimioi attack. MHSRIP. We all thrived after independence, rising through the ranks in the security services, or in public or private sectors. The war hardened, enlightened, and empowered us.

On my flight to Ethiopia in 1978, I read an article in Newsweek magazine. Father Prosar, the principal of St Augustine's, was quoted saying the war had robbed them of some of their most brilliant and promising students, including me.

Then my father was called by the Headmaster. He was refunded all the fees he had paid that year. Not only was I one of the brightest and most disciplined students, but I also had a poor medical history.

At Mutambara Mission, we saw a few relatives and friends. They pleaded to join us, but we decided not to add more risks. When we asked for directions to the border, we proceeded into the unknown territory of the Eastern Highlands, the Chimanimani Mountains. Around 8 pm, we decided to camp in a donga. We kept turns to stand guard. Just before sunrise, we came across a tribesman herding donkeys. He pointed us in the right direction but warned us about the Rhodesian Soldiers on patrol. Around 10 am, we arrived at the boundary fence. On the Mozambican side, there was a eucalyptus plantation. About two kilometers inside, we were suddenly surrounded by armed Frelimo soldiers.

They interrogated us. We told them we had come to join our brothers waging war against the Boers. After a day, they arranged transport for us to be transferred to the main camp, about 10 kilometers away at Rutanda, opposite Cashel Valley, a Frelimo training camp with Tanzanian military instructors. There was a civilian official who wrote down our details. Within days, our numbers started swelling as other students from other schools joined us, including another group of 5 from Bocha who were a bit older than us.

When we were about 15, the official drove us to Chimioi, the provincial capital. He left us with Mozambican Intelligence. There I met my childhood friend, and now best friend, Aaron Gwasira. He had just finished O levels at Waddilove and had also crossed together with Rejoice Mbanje, later to be the wife of Minister Ernest Kadungure's wife, and I were taken to the Zanu logistics base in Chimoio. The number was now close to a hundred, mostly school children from different secondary schools like me. We knew each other; in those days, schools were few and we used to meet for sports and other activities.

At that base were also casualties from the Nyazonia Massacre who had recovered and were waiting to be taken back to the camps. For the first time, it became clear to me that what we had read in newspapers about Rhodesians raiding guerrilla camps in Mozambique was a reality. We were then ferried in batches by lorries delivering supplies to the Doroi Refugee Camp.

A kilometer into the camp was the security checkpoint. We were searched and stripped. For the older recruits, the interrogation was tougher, with screening for spies and infiltrators. Some of the methods and tactics used bordered on superstition and cruelty. Those security guys had a 90% success rate of flushing out traitors. However, there were a few cases of innocent people wrongly accused of being spies. When the security guys spotted a smartly dressed recruit, especially one of those migrant workers coming from Wenela, South Africa, they would either sweet-talk or violently take away his nice jeans and watches.

We watched activities in the camp from a distance. We were still under security scrutiny, not yet free. I was very impressed seeing battalions of men and women marching, singing, and generally in high spirits. Occasionally, you would see a face you recognize but were not yet allowed to talk with him or her. Worse, if that person greeted or spoke with you, both would be in hot water. It was only on the third day that I knew Doroi was in fact a refugee camp, not a training camp. After the security clearance, we were released to a commander. He arranged us regimentally into sections, platoons, companies, then battalions.

Section to platoon commanders, their Deputies, Political Commissars, medics, security, logistics assistants, were randomly selected amongst the recruits. Senior ranks, company, detachment, and battalion level were seniors who were assigned to us. At the camp command level, mostly were trained personnel. Then a few members of the General Staff. In some instances, at the top was a member of the High Command or Central Committee.

We paraded twice a day in our formations. Roll calls, numbers counted, any desertion or sickness were reported. In the morning, we were assigned different duties. There was only one meal per day. The three months, from September to November 1976, I was at Doroi, the diet was a half ration of sadza and powdered milk. When it rained, the milk would be diluted to just water. Anything salty was gold. Girls started having a rare disease associated with malnutrition called HURRICCANES, hiccups, and funny uncontrolled walking and stammering.

The routine was in the morning military drills, duties to go and gather firewood, or to help build wooden barracks,and afternoons political orientation. At some stage, we did mock military training conducted by comrade Chihambakwe, later Honorable Moses Mwenge. I enjoyed political lessons. During the national grievance session, each and every one of us was given a chance to voice his or her experiences. Some older cadres had very interesting stories to share. This was punctuated by singing and dancing. This was in 1976, the fashion was Bump jive and mujibha styles.

Morris Muzvuzvu was promoted into the medical corps. Every promotion came with its own benefits, better and more food, flexible time, more freedom, better clothing, a better chance of being selected for training, and if at Company Command level and above, admission to the TABLE, or officers' mess.

After 2 months, I was promoted to be a platoon security officer. The duties were in the evening, taking turns to guard the camp peripherals and important posts like command post, kitchens, clinics, libraries, etc., escort VIPs. During the day, we would go out on patrols up to a 10-kilometer radius of the camp, looking out for the enemy and general intelligence gathering. The Selius Scouts and Remanos renegades were always trying to enter our camps, looking out and capturing deserters.

And there were comrades who stole others' clothes and items and bartered with the Mozambican locals for food, cigarettes, beer, and drugs. The security guys were major culprits. We were coached on how to approach a peasant.

We were coached on how to approach a peasant, kindly ask for any intelligence leads, and then politely request a meal in exchange for some items. Since I had not consumed beer, cigarettes, or dagga, I eventually left the security department and drifted back to the commissariat. It was more creative and interesting, especially if your political instructor was a former student of Chitepo College.

Come November 1976, there was a heavy influx of senior commanders during the peak of the Zipa era and leading up to the Geneva Conference. For us in the commissariat, it was then briefing after briefing. At that time, the influx of new recruits had intensified and signs of a health pandemic were showing. It was estimated that the population at Dorio was around 100,000 at the time. Movements out of Doroi or any other refugee camp for training were very minimal. At most, 10 to 50 people at a time were taken to Tembwe or Chimioi for training. Mostly, it was those with special skills like drivers, secretaries, nurses, engineers, or extra fit guys to be crash program trained for special missions on the war front.

Then one afternoon in November 1976, the Chief of Operations, Rex Nhongo, drove into the camp with a convoy of brand new lorries, donated from Sweden. He was in very high spirits and announced that 10,000 cadres were going for training in Tanzania. The coming weeks day and night were filled with lorries carrying comrades out for training. First, it was survivors of the Nyazonia Massacre who had fully recovered. Only when a battalion was away was it their turn; it was announced that the required number had been reached. Luckily, after a week, the then Director of Training, Parker Chipowera, came and said 500 more were needed, but there was no transport. I was among those asked to run to the Gondola Train station, 20 kilometers from the camp. However, a few days prior, I had developed a tropical ulcer, a very big sore on my ankle. I didn't care. On the road with others, after 10 kilometers, my leg became so painful. I fell out and rested. Parker and his team, who were following behind in their Landrover, saw me. They gave me a lift. I thought they were going to take me back to the camp. Moreover, I was a bit underage for training, being one month shy of my 16th birthday, and had deteriorated due to a poor diet.

To this day, I always remind Cde Parker, now a senior agronomist at ZfC, how he saved me. We boarded the train at Gondola around 8 pm. By that time, my leg had swollen and was painful. When we reached Beira, I was almost invalid. I was ferried on a stretcher to the Hospital at the Air Base. In the meantime, people were being arranged into groups to board planes to Tanzania.

At Beira, we met other cadres from other refugee camps: Chibawawa, Tembwe, Xai.

There was a small group of officers from Chimioi headquarters who were to be course leaders and commissars. On Christmas day 1976, a group of 700 comrades from Tanzania arrived at Beira airbase. They were the last group to be trained at Mgagao, and that's where we were previously earmarked to go.

Then Cde Mark Dube arrived, deputizing Teura Ropa as the camp commander at Chibawawa. His other visitors were Tongogara and Mayor Urimbo. Comrade Tongo cried and briefed us about the Geneva Conference, how he is now having problems being welcomed back by the Zipa commanders. Then 1,000 of us, plus our few commissars, were then transported back to Dondo, a Frelimo camp, 20km from Beira. Our Chief political commissar was Comrade Top Ten, later Senior Permanent Secretary Justin Mupanhanga. By then, I had fully recovered and was promoted to platoon commander.

As it was a Frelimo camp, food was plentiful, and most basics were very available. The routine was drills in the morning then political lessons or discussions in the afternoon for the whole 6 months. We studied all the works of Lenin, Trotsky, Mao, Art of War, etc. We had daily briefings from the Frelimo commanders as it was the time of the 3rd Frelimo congress.

In June 1977, a delegation from Headquarters headed by Mayor Urimbo arrived. He said we had been deliberately quarantined. Tanzania, Mgagao was no longer a training camp. All other camps in Mozambique were going through a significant inter-party crisis. The Vashandi Rebellion or so, most commanders were arrested, demoted, or had deserted, and some even killed. But now all was well, half of us were going for training at Tembwe, the other half to Chimoio. The following day a convoy of buses came, I was in the group going to Chimoio. It was debatable whether we were trained personnel or not based on how we were dressed, fit, and disciplined.

There was a new, larger training base being established 10 kilometers away, Takawira 2, or Taks by the river. By this time, the population at Doroi had swelled to more than 150,000. The time is remembered for disease and hunger. There was a battalion of very strong able-bodied men "Battalion Z," commanded by

Mahomohomoi, now Chigwedere, formed specifically to carry out tough duties like burials, averaging 30 to 50 per day. I lost my cousin, a classmate from the village who was born with disabilities but had bravely volunteered to go and fight for his country. PETER MABIKA, May his soul rest in peace.

Cadres from 'Battalion Z" were taken from Doroi to construct this base. As the population at Dorio was over 150,000, the chances for someone to go for training were slim except for those with special skills sought after by other departments of the party. Only the creative and determined ones resorted to manoeuvre. That's walking up to 25 km from Doroi or 150km from Chibawawa to Chimoio or Tembwe for training. If one is unlucky, they may be intercepted by the camp security patrols and mistaken as a deserter. Alternatively, upon arrival in Chimioi, depending on the duty officer's mood or the situation, they may be put on the next ration truck back to Doroi and face imprisonment. The fortunate few are sent to Takawira 2 to assist in constructing the new camp and receive further training.

At the Takawira 2 training base, when I arrived, there were only a few officers supervising the work. The commander was Comrade Martin Ndhlovu, who later became the longest-serving ADC to President Mugabe. He immediately took me on as his secretary, and I was excused from the manual work of constructing barracks, training grounds, and kits, etc. I moved into better accommodation and received my meals at the table. I was now a mid-ranking officer.

Soon all the training staff, led by Comrade Chocha, the later Director of Training and future ZRP Commissioner General, arrived and training started in earnest. Only a few recruits were taken from refugee camps because the numbers had naturally filled up.

During training, a group of carefully selected cadres called "Company 144" was chosen. I was among them. As I was young, there was a section within it called the "Red Guards," and I was the commander. Soon after finishing training, about 30 of us were selected for a mission abroad. The group was mixed, from high ranking to lowest. We were taken to the Chimioi Chamuka Intelligence base for briefing.

For about two weeks, we were taught in-depth party structures and party policies. Coincidentally, this was when the Zanu conference transformed RG Mugabe from Secretary General to President, with Muzenda as Deputy and Tekere as Secretary General. We were assigned to close security and secretarial duties. I came to know most of the Central Committee and High Command officers on a personal basis.

After the conference, we went with Tekere's former wife, Jane Mujeni, who was a professional photographer, in the late Comrade Mandeyas' bus to Chimioi town for passport applications. The following day at 6 am, we were told to return to the Takawira 2 base. With the same bus, which tragically was later burned by the Rhodesians during the Chimioi attack, we arrived at the morning parade time. The duty officer didn't assign us duties yet as we needed to settle down. Within minutes, all was horror.

Jock Mallock used to fly his AFFREIGHTAIR DC 8 plane past the camp, so we thought it was a routine civilian passenger plane. However, planes were everywhere - Dakotas dropping paratroopers, helicopter gunships. The attack had begun. But

Takawira 2 was a training base, and more or less everybody was armed. And they had some heavy arms for training. The enemy retreated after less than 5 minutes, moving to concentrate on less defended bases 10 km away. Bases for women, schools, elderly, hospitals, logistics, production, transport, etc.

I rushed to the armory and was given a gun. Now we organized escape routes. Nearby was a base of vane Sekuru, Elderly, and Spirit mediums. We started meeting people running away from the main camp. Some were injured, some were in shock, including men, women, and children. We covered up the escape route, helping the injured up to Chimioi town. There was a stadium set up as a gathering point, a reception area. That day and the following, there was heavy fighting all over in the direction of Chimioi camp. Casualties were coming in. On the third day, we, the trained personnel, were driven back to the camp. Our first task was to rescue the injured who were still alive. We rescued Mrs. Tekere from a pit latrine. Then came the burial of the dead. At my tender age, this was quite traumatic. I recognized a few comrades: Doit, an albino girl, one of the commanders at Dorio; Comrade Taurai, my first political instructor; Cde Moi, my battalion Commander in Beira; and home boys and girls Catherine and Cuthbert, whom I grew up with at Musaringo. One of the only six casualties at Takawira 2 was none other than my cousin, Clifford, who crossed the border with me on the same day from St Faiths. May Their Souls Rest in Peace.

After the burial, most people had rendezvoused at Gondola. I sneaked into Mumango Operations base wanting to go to the war front. Unfortunately, I had eaten poisoned food rations and ended up admitted at Chimioi General Hospital. When I recovered, I was earmarked to go to Doroi Refugee camp as a junior trained commander. I didn't like that, so at the nearest opportunity, I jumped into a supplies truck to the training camp. I joined a group of 30 other comrades sent to China to attend a youth conference at Canton, spending over three months training in heavy artillery, politics, and intelligence.

When we came back around mid-April, cadres in training had moved a camp near Pungwe River, now offering specialized training. I joined in and was assigned to special small arms, light machine gun, and recently introduced Lancers - Rifle Launched grenades. We moved on to an operation base near Villa Paiva, Villa Gouveya in the Pungwe area.

There was a convergence of forces now. The groups from Tanzania were easily identified with their khaki uniforms, black boots, who spoke and drilled in Swahili. They practiced a very heavy drill, semi-conventional warfare. We from China, the minority, had Chinese green cotton uniforms, matching green caps with red star badges, and green canvas shoes. Mao literature books. The local-trained were very thin but had good endurance, with torn clothes, no standard uniform. They were streetwise, especially at the kitchen for extra rations. The most difficult group was those coming from the war front. They were identified by wearing the latest fashions of clothes found in Indian shops, green, black, or brown Revolution trousers, matching shirts with as many pockets as possible, and farmer's shoes or Super pro shoes. They wore big veranda cowboy hats and slung their guns at a certain angle, not in any standard military book. They were stubborn and defied standard routine orders, demanded special treatments especially if one was injured in the battlefield. As commanders, it was difficult to blend these forces. But at the end of the day, the job was done. The war was waged. Later on, towards the end, there were also groups trained mostly in intelligence from countries like Romania and Yugoslavia.

The Mazees, the elderly, were given lighter duties and occasionally sent to hunt game to supplement their meager rations. Some were experts in traditional medicines. This group included the Spirit Mediums, who one needed to approach with care. Lastly, those not yet trained tried to impress at any given opportunity.

TO ETHIOPIA

I was waiting to be deployed to the front as a senior officer at the Detachment level. Still not yet 18, I was headhunted by Director of Manpower Planning, Comrade Shumba, later known as Ambassador Mvundura, along with Denny Murimo. The interviewer was none other than Cde Chee, Ambassador Christopher Mutswangwa. He introduced himself, surprisingly having read my personal file. He mentioned that he was in the same class with my brother at St Augustine's, and they together broke the national record, earning a bursary as the first African students to study law at the University of Rhodesia. He didn't doubt my intellect and told me I was to go on a mission where a very high IQ was a prerequisite. I pleaded that I wanted to go to the front, but Comrade Denny, short-tempered as he was, threatened me with imprisonment. A few other select individuals and I jumped into a Land Rover en route to Maputo.

In Maputo, we were introduced to Cde Ngangana as Deputy Head of Production. The head of the department was Cde Peter Baya, a Central Committee member who was seriously ill and died a few days later; we buried him in Maputo. The next was Cde Shamuyarira; no title was given. He briefed us that an important man was coming from Ethiopia and we must present ourselves with the highest decorum and discipline. We were all to have nice haircuts, no big hats, no jeans, no t-shirts, and no slanted English. He briefed Cde Dzingai Mtumbuka, who was the secretary for Education. I thought maybe we were being recruited for Teacher's Training. The next day we were taken to a military hospital, accompanied by Cde Gertrude Mutasa, for medical examinations.

A few days later, the gentleman arrived. He looked like a colored or Egyptian or Arab or Black American. He was introduced as Colonel Asrat, Training Director of Ethiopian Airlines. He was a no-nonsense man but treated me as a son. First, we were given a past school-leaving examination paper written in Nigeria that year, i.e., O level Math, an English paper, and an aptitude scholastic test. I don't know how much I scored. I just overheard the colonel and Cde Shamuyarira discussing something about me and two others being a bit too young. The Colonel said not to worry; this isn't an academy, we take them young and groom them. The next day, we were asked to fill out passport forms. Half of us filled in British Passports as "British Subjects", while I and a few others filled out Mozambican ones. I wonder why they wasted our time; the only section we filled was our date of birth. We were later given passports with assumed names that we had to memorize and adopt. This time, we were shortlisted to 20. The next set of forms varied; some had letterheads from UNESCO, some from UNPD, while mine was from the International Universities Exchange Fund, P.O. xxx Geneva, with the caption 'Providing educational assistance for refugees from Southern Africa.' We filled in our personal details based on the information provided for us on the passport application. For the next section, College/university, we were instructed to fill in

'Ethiopian Airlines Aviation School' for the duration from '1st August 1978 to 30th July 1980' for the course 'Airframes and Powerplant Systems.'

I admit, I was confused and lost. In the coming weeks, we spent time moving about in Maputo town. Occasionally, we would sneak to where cadres enrolled at Mondlane University were staying. Among them were my former commissar Top Ten, Bara, my company commander at Doroi, who had come to join the war from Swaziland with three pairs of suits, and Carlos Bvuma, who had just finished writing his first play, 'The People Are Invincible,' satirizing the 1978 Abele Muzorewa Internal Settlement. With Top Ten as the director, we performed the drama to a group of African Diplomats in Maputo.

One day, twenty of us were herded to the clothing stores, where thousands of used clothes were packed into bales. Each of us was asked to choose four trousers, two shirts, and one jacket. We were then taken to Mr. Populous' shop, the long-time chair of the Zimbabwe-Mozambique Friendship Association. Each of us chose a pair of socks, underwear, and shoes. Two people shared each suitcase that was bought.

We were then taken to the Zanu Head Offices in Maputo. Waiting outside, I saw my friend Aaron Gwasira, also known as Zambe Nyika. He was accompanying the Gaza Field Commander, Freddy Matanga. The Zimbabwe News photographer was there, taking pictures. Pictures of Zambe and me in war attire were later published in many editions of party magazines. Subsequently, the Secretary General, Edgar Tekere, asked us to board the waiting cars for a direct drive to Maputo Airport. To signify the importance of our mission, the SG himself handed us our passports, air tickets, and $50 each. He gave a small speech of encouragement and reminded us to always remember the revolutionary goals.

Our next stop was Dar es Salaam. The Ethiopian Airlines plane arrived, and we were greeted by Comrades Dzingai Mtumbuka and John Chimbande, who was the Chief Representative in Tanzania, and my former commander, Cde Dragon, now introduced as the New Chief Representative in Ethiopia. They were coming from Addis and reassured us that they had secured our places and spoke highly of the airlines.

We arrived in Addis around mid-day. Ethiopia was in the middle of a civil war at the time, embroiled in the Red Terror, the Ogaden War with Somalia, and a war with Eritrea. As soon as we disembarked and started walking on the tarmac, we saw two guys speaking in Shona. The first was Santos Moyo, who greeted us in Ndebele and then in Shona. Then came Charles Salad Samuriwo with his wide smile, saying, "Comrades, welcome to Ethiopia."

The Aviation Academy's hostels are within the airport compound. At the immigration point, we were met by the Acting Training Manager, Ato Tsegaye. As it was a weekend, I think he was a bit bored. He escorted us to the Immigration Desk, presented our student visas, and declared that we were refugees from Zimbabwe. He delegated Charles to take us to our dormitories and show us around.

About 20 comrades were waiting there. A month before us, another group of 10 had come from Zambia, and about 15 from the UK and other countries who ended up in Ethiopia by other means. We were the second group from the war front and the first from Mozambique. Our group was a mixture of Zanla, Zipra, and other non-combatant cadres.

Once we were all settled in, we changed our money into local currency and collected our weekly allowances. We also secured our passes. We hiked to town to meet with those working in the party office and international organizations like the UN and OAU. Comrade Stalin Mau Mau, the most senior among us, briefed us about life in Addis and Ethiopia in general.

We started classes. The first semester was comprised of academic subjects like Maths, Physics, Technical Drawing, Aviation Law, Aerodynamics, and Material Science. For each subject, the pass mark was 70%. Failure meant immediate expulsion. Luckily, we all passed. The academy had students from all over Africa, Arab countries, the Mediterranean, and locals.

The Ethiopians, the students, and junior instructors spoke with an accent that was difficult to understand. The older instructors, mostly retired army officers who had trained abroad, adopted an American accent. The Ethiopians loved their raw meat and spiced and hot food. For the first three months, I settled for tea and buns only. This affected my health and led to food poisoning.

Just before the next stage of training, I was called to the company clinic. My medical reports were not up to standard. At all operation bases and in Maputo, I had mastered the art of concealing my injuries or any minor illness. Now, with the use of X-ray, laboratories, scans, and highly specialized aviation doctors, I was finally caught...

On top of the prescription, a referral to Empress Zewditi Seventh Day Memorial Hospital was given. Colonel Asrat had already signed his consent as a guardian. I was scheduled to undergo surgery in the abdomen.

I didn't have much trouble locating the hospital as it was next to the Stalin Mau Maus hotel. I was given a private ward in the Surgical Department. It was during the peak of the Odagen War and the military had commandeered the hospital. Badly injured soldiers were scattered all over the floors, most of them in great pain. If you've ever been to a military or prison clinic, you'll know that the doctors tend to give orders without listening to the patients. It was traumatic.

The ward I was in was shared by two girls: Almaz, a university student, and Desta, who was studying at an agricultural college. They could speak some English. The nurses and staff mostly didn't like speaking in English, and my Amharic was still very poor at the time.

On the day of my operation, the doctor, who was Russian/Soviet, and his assistant, a Cuban lady, didn't speak a word of English. The Ethiopian anesthetist acted as the interpreter. He examined me without even reading my case history and directed me to the theater. I walked there on my own, laid down on the operation table, and then the Anesthetist came. He made a joke and then, the next thing I knew, I woke up.

Day 3 in the hospital brought surprise visitors. It was during the Malta talks, so en route, the leaders of the Patriot Front, Joshua Nkomo and Robert Mugabe, and their delegations passed through Addis. They were told that a comrade was admitted to the hospital and decided to visit me.

I was discharged, went for a medical examination, and was cleared. But I missed a month's worth of lessons. Surprisingly, I caught up and graduated cum laude. My name is engraved on the Ethiopian Airlines Aviation Academy roll of honor for class 21A of 1980.

Life in Ethiopia was filled with studying, humor, and camaraderie. Our scholarships were generous, and we were also given weekly pocket money from the Airlines. Beautiful and welcoming girls were plentiful.

Later, we were joined by more cadres, including girls and some for management training. I, Stalin Organ Masimbah, as the youngest member of the Patriot Front cadres at the time, was tasked to present our petition to William Eleki, then Secretary General of the Organization of African Unity, stating, "We, as fighters of the Patriotic Front, do not recognize the Muzorewa Rhodesia-Zimbabwe internal settlement. The struggle continues. We will fight to the bitter end." ALUTA CONTINUA.

In 1979, Bob Marley and the Wailers came to Ethiopia, not to perform but to meet with us. It was during this meeting that he got the inspiration to compose the song "Zimbabwe". Captain Alex Makanda still has some of the photos.

HOMECOMING

After the signing of the agreement, their first stop was Addis. General Tongo booked a room at the Hilton Hotel and invited us to an all-night party. A few days later, a telex message arrived stating that two of the members at the party, comrades Jomo and

Embassy, must board the first plane to Beira to join the first group of 50 commanders heading to Harare.

A ceasefire was signed, Zanu Pf. won. We were now free to write home. I wrote and received a few letters. One was from my father, saying he thought I had long died, for the day I left St Faiths, near Penhalonga, Rhodesians had killed dozens of school children trying to cross to Mozambique. Also, at a nearby village, there was a fierce battle and one of our relatives said she had just cooked food for me, fearing I was one of the dead. He said he is now teaching at Gora School in Mhondoro. My brother Timothy wrote and sent a few photographs with family members at his graduation from the University of Rhodesia. He said he is now employed as a public prosecutor and one of our cousins, Shepard Gwasira, was amongst the first group of ex-combatants to be integrated into the Police force.

Unfortunately, our sponsor, International Universities Fund, was now defunct. The new government sent the then finance minister, Enos Nkala, and the Secretary for Manpower Planning, Dr. Ibbo Mandaza, to Ethiopia. They were able to secure alternative funding from UNDP.

It was time to come home. Our Mozambique and British Passports had expired. At that time, by rotation, I was the Student Governor. We approached UNHCR and were issued with Stateless person travel documents. Initially, I was supposed to travel to Salisbury on the 8th August 1980. That was the day of the inaugural Ethiopian Airlines flight to Harare. The flight was full of senior airline staff wanting to establish offices and businesses. The same was true the following Tuesday. It was only at the end of August that we finally landed in Harare.

My father, coming from Mhondoro, and my mother and other family members from the village, after twice not seeing me on the flight, decided to go back. The day I came, there was nobody to welcome me. But others, especially those with families in Harare, had big welcoming parties, signing "Mauya Mauya Comrade, Hamuchadzoka".

Some of the cadres who returned home earlier were already there in Air Rhodesia uniforms. I had all my clothes, documents, and books in my flight case. After the uninterested white immigration officer stamped and tore my stateless person paper/passport, I went out of the airport building and boarded the first available taxi.

I had a note with the address 6992, Unit J, Seke. I didn't know where this was. I used to read in African Times newspapers that Seke was one of the tribal Chiefs. After leaving the airport parking area, the driver turned right, but traffic to town was straight on. After the Airbase, we entered some isolated farming areas. Ten kilometers further, we got to a highway with much traffic. Another five kilometers and there was still no sign of any town or settlement. The taxi meter was dropping $ and cents, and I was penniless. The driver asked, "Are you coming from the war? Why didn't you go to the assembly point barracks?"

Eventually, we came to Chikwanha Shopping center. My father, in one of his letters, had written that his sister had an accident and died at Chirandahuo Squatter camp near Chikwanha. Then we Nyatsime College, I remember the names Charles Samuriwo and Hertz. They said they went to Nyatsime College. We passed a highly populated area, then a fairly new suburb, not much populated. The driver then started making inquiries about where he could find house number 6992. He passed through a communal village setup, then stopped at the last house. He hooted.

My brother, Innocent, had come a month earlier. He had been studying in Kenya but aborted his course to come to independent Zimbabwe. Innocent was chatting with some neighbors. At that time, he was the Zanu Pf Youth leader. At last, I was home. These guys opened the taxi boot expecting some luggage. I only had my flight case. After the greetings, the driver waited patiently for his fare. I had a small consultation with Innocent. Luckily, next door lived Mr. Ruboko, a court interpreter who worked with my brother Timothy at the courts. He was home. Innocent talked with him. The fare was $15.00. Mr. Rukobo paid and I was home.

When the war had intensified in the eastern districts, my father was forced to abandon teaching. Schools were closed, teachers were targeted, and every new group of comrades asked for donations of jeans and watches from teachers. The Rhodesians equally targeted teachers as supporters of freedom fighters.

But in 1978, he couldn't help it. Timothy was at University, Innocent was in boarding school at St Augustine, and Tambisa was at Hartzell. He had to find employment. First, he was employed part-time by an insurance company. Then a colleague told him that in Mhondoro, as there was not yet a war zone, experienced teachers like him were in demand. In the meantime, he secured a house from Chitungwiza town co.

One weekend, Timothy came. He had a small Renault 4 car. He took me around to see relatives in different locations. My aunt Netty was a manager at a whites-only creche in Cheryl Road, Avondale. Then Uncle Furamera was the Zanu Pf Mashona provincial PC. At that time, the province included Mashonaland East and West and Harare. He had offices at Ottawa house and a party issue vehicle. He was a jovial giant of a man. He had been a delegate of the Peoples Movement, a Zanu Pf affiliate, to the Lancaster conference. He started boasting to his colleagues, "See my nephew? I facilitated his scholarship to Ethiopia, now he is one of our pioneer Aviators."

On Sunday evening, when Timothy was going back to Bulawayo where he was now working at Tredgold Building Courts, he gave me some money as pocket money and for travel to the village. But he warned me. He said that as a Public Prosecutor, he was dealing with cases of ex-combatants arrested when in over-indulgence or for desertion from units, and sometimes referred to as dissidents on a daily basis. So, I must be careful. Also, kidnappings of ex-combatants as remnants of The Selous Scouts were still common.

Monday morning, I went to the Musika bus station. Buses were few then. I hitchhiked to Rusape. The driver, Mr. Ruredzo, was the father of Timothy's friend at the University. He himself had spent many years in political detention. He offered me the front seat of his Peugeot 404 station wagon. He talked all the way to Rusape.

In Rusape, the first person I saw was my classmate from form 1R and form 3, Everett Mtungwazi. He had just finished his form 6 at Goromonzi. He was very excited. I had a framed picture of comrades coming from training in Tanzania. He invited me to go and see his parents who had taught with my father a long time ago.

I proceeded to Nyazura. Things had completely changed. A new highway connecting to Dorowa had been built. But the mountains near the village could still be seen about 12km away. I negotiated to hire a car.

Apparently, the guys were going a bit further down. After about 30 minutes, I was in the village. They dropped me about 200 meters from the homesteads and continued on their way. Whoever saw me started singing and ululating; within minutes, a crowd had formed to welcome their son. Among the first to come was my uncle and friends coming from a local beer party. They asked whose car it was. I said it was some people from the village down there. Then they asked how much I had paid. I said $5. They claimed that was too much and suggested we chase down the car and demand change, hoping to buy an extra mug of beer. To me, the fare seemed very reasonable.

Then my grandfather came. Earlier, his younger brother, a bishop of a sect, had said some words of ancestral worship, stating that the spirits had protected our son, who had fought and shed his blood for the country.

My father was at his garden, so he was the last to see me. He wept uncontrollably upon seeing me. Now he was 50 years old. My grandfather, a no-nonsense man, shouted at him that we should rejoice, not cry.

I went to my father's house. Drinks were served, and I was first given leftover meal (munya). I hadn't eaten sadza for 3 years. First in Mozambique, after the food poisoning, Dr. Ushehwekunze, our medic, had recommended only a light diet, mostly spaghetti. Then in Ethiopia, their staple food is injera. That day, I was in pain, as if my stomach had burst.

After the greeting formalities, as we are Manyikas, very traditionalists, no matter how many of us there are, the request to salute circulated from the most junior to the most senior. When the senior acknowledged the salute, the response went down again through the same channel. A mistake or wrong protocol would result in the process being repeated. This process could take up to 30 minutes. Then we clapped in the correct sequence.

At about 5 pm, the welcome party started in earnest. A bull was slaughtered, along with numerous goats and chickens. Crates of cool drinks from the local shops and dozens of loaves of bread were brought in. Even though my parents don't like alcohol, beer was plentiful. Young brides of the village were assigned to do the cooking, while those who happened to have married our sisters did the manual work, finding firewood, fetching water, making makeshift tents, the most senior among them acted as directors of ceremonies, making public announcements. The word spread so fast that, on that day, I saw relatives -- some for the first time -- who had traveled up to 30 kilometres away to come and see me. During the ceasefire, buses and trucks were seen on the nearby highway, taking comrades to assembly points. Afterward, some people would follow to locate their relatives. When a group of ladies asked my mother to check for relatives at the assembly points, she adamantly refused. By then, I was already writing from Ethiopia.

Seeing me, some people didn't believe it was really me. Plus, I was coming from town, not from the city camps as they expected a guerrilla to dress.

The next day, I had a one-on-one talk with my father about my career plans. He suggested I go and finish school. I argued, "But now I have a higher diploma in Aeronautics, why should I?" The next day, we went into town and, in an Indian shop where he had an account, purchased two suits, two shirts, a pair of shoes, and a necktie. To this day, those Indian shop owners address me as 'Teacher's son' whenever they see me.

My father offered to send me back to school, even if it meant selling off some cows, as all my siblings have degrees. I found this to be unfair. I was earning about five times more than a school teacher, plus he had a big extended family to look after. Not to disappoint him, I approached a section in the Ministry of Education administered by comrades Fay Chung and Mushatagotsi Chitopfu that funded further education for ex-combatants.

A few days later, I returned to Salisbury. First, I had to find out what had happened to my colleagues. Most had gone to their parents or relatives in rural areas. A few who had no relatives in Harare were staying at Medical Arts in Mt Pleasant, where senior Zanla commanders were housed.

We made arrangements to meet at the Ministry of Manpower Planning offices and filled in applications for employment. When we came back after a week, the government made an experiment. We saw an Airforce bus parked outside with its white driver.

The last agreed solution was that we would be retrained and have accelerated promotions. We agreed to this. When it was time to write trade tests, the forms were from South Africa. The options for race were 'White', 'Afrikaans', 'Asian', 'Colored', and 'Others'. The chances of passing were slim.

BAPTISM TO H-TOWN

Regrettably, I got to know Harare late. By coincidence, I had been to and lived in bigger cities before and experienced more metropolitan life. It was through the collaborations of my brother Timothy, my long-time childhood and war-time friend Aaron, and two younger friends Richard Wakatama and Richard Tanyanyiwa that I saw the bright light of the Sunshine City.

I joined Air Zimbabwe as a trainee graduate apprentice Engineer. To KLM, it was just a paid holiday. The textbooks and all training material were just the same as at Ethiopian Airlines.

Back at Air Zimbabwe, I had the option not to work in the Workshops. The pay was a bit less than those in Line Maintenance and hangars. It was an 8 to 5 job, always clean, with white dust coats and access to the staff canteen. There, you mingled with administrative staff, mostly ladies, and air hostesses on training. Money was not a problem. After all, my brother came back with the latest BMW car in town from RSA and had connections in Johannesburg, so whatever I wanted was easy to get.

I was to have a trainee under me, who happened to be none other than Richard Tanyanyiwa, a boy from the ghetto. He was born in Mbare. Having completed his A-levels at Fletcher and CIS, he was concurrently studying Aircraft Engineering. His two elder brothers owned an ivory craft shop and managed their books. They had purchased him a Mini Cooper, a fashionable car at the time, especially for a first-year apprentice. His father was a school teacher in Mbare.

The first time I asked him for his address, he told me to go to Beatrice Cottages and simply ask for "The House, 1 Nyazika Road." I made it a routine that if Richard didn't bring his Mini Cooper, I would drop him off after work. Mostly on weekends, after my shopping, I would pick up my friend Aaron, provided he was off duty.

Aaron was now employed by Zesa as a generating shift control supervisor at the Power Station. In those days, there were no cell phones; the routine was to go to your date's house, park your car 3 blocks away, find a small boy to send a message, and she would come out. I would tell her to get ready, come back after an hour, and then leave. Meanwhile, I would drive to the house. Before Richard could come out, one or two older boys would approach me, asking for a cigarette or a coin to buy Chibuku. They would praise my car, and if I refused their requests, they would puncture my tires. I would then have to pay them to repair the damage. Aaron always reminded me how the boys from Beatrice Cottages used to belittle us from the villages at boarding schools.

Our other friend was Richard Wakatama, who was a rival to Richard Tanyanyiwa. Tanyanyiwa would narrate how they were surprised when the Wakatamas returned from America. While still residing in Mbare, they attended a Pentecostal Church where the entire family, all wearing watches, would sit in the front row. The father, Pius, spoke with an accent. His sister, Mrs. Dsouza, ran the most sophisticated shebeen in Mbare at that time.

Richard Wakatama was privileged. His father trained as a teacher and then went to America to study Theological Journalism. His mother, Winnie Ndoro, came from a middle-class family and was an Insurance Executive. During the Rhodesia-Zimbabwe era, his father was appointed to a number of boards including Art. Richard had the opportunity to be among the first group to attend multi-racial schools. He was well-connected.

I was introduced to him by Timothy when Mrs. Wakatama sold Aaron and me Old Mutual insurance policies. During the "Know Your Customer" questionnaire, she was impressed with us, so she didn't mind or even encouraged her son to hang around with us. On Fridays and Saturdays, Richard Wakatama would come to my flat and sleep over, but on Sundays, he was obligated to attend church. Wherever there was a party, Richard knew about it. If we gate-crashed, Richard knew someone inside. At that time, my friend Aaron had bought a Datsun 140Y.

The problem with Richard was his propensity for high life tastes, but he didn't have the money. Especially on Saturday evenings or Sunday mornings, he would ask to be driven home in Tynwald. At that time, town only extended as far as Warren Park 1, and Tynwald was still a farming area. At home, I was his shield to his parents, reassuring them that he was not up to any mischief. His father was a literature man and would start lecturing on different subjects, then invite me to his kitchen or garden, show me around and explain every recipe he could make.

Chapter Eleven: The Kingdom Man

By Nigel Chanakira

My name is Nigel Muranganwa Kudzayi Chanakira. I was born at Harare Central Hospital, where my mother worked as a nurse. She was a registered nurse by profession. She trained at Mpilo and then my dad, on the other hand, was a businessman and he's still a businessman. My mom has retired. My dad worked with his brothers, and they ran a business; Modern Express Company, which incorporated buses as well as shops both in the townships and then in the rural areas, particularly Seke, which is the area that they were raised in. They themselves were children of a polygamous family, whereby my great-grandfather was the pioneer bus owner and operator in Southern Rhodesia.
So the first bus company that was ever registered by a black person in Southern Rhodesia was registered and owned by Chanakira, and so from that perspective, we have a strong lineage in our family and I would say that I'm a third generation businessman and as a consequence, my dad has tremendous influence in my life as I grew up, because he was a businessman. The attributes that I respect about my dad are that he was independent, he was a Christian, and that he expressed himself freely on matters of politics and self-determination. The whole independence struggle was dear to his heart. So, he not only talked about things, but he put his money where his mouth was.

He and his brothers funded the struggle - they supported "Vakomana" (guerillas) as it was, and they took groceries and clothing to them using our buses, using the shops in, Seke, Chihota, and Nyamweeda communal lands, and they also plied bus routes all the way through to Bulawayo.

My great uncle, my dad's eldest brother Kupara Chanakira, was also a great influence on me. They called him "MK"; I share the same initials, Nigel "MK" Chanakira, and he eventually inherited the bus company. I must add that the bus company was originally just a lorry that had benches, and it plied its trade between Seke and Mbare and, therefore, that ultimately became the Modern Omnibus Company which they ran. They ended up, I think, with about 30 buses and several shops. Again, they were pioneers.

They had the first of the first shopping malls ever built in Rhodesia or Zimbabwe at Lusaka in Highfields, and my dad, having been a carpenter by training, was responsible for building the shops, you know, shelving them and making sure that they were in good working order. He then managed the shops that they had.

I grew up in an environment where these businesspersons had great love for each other. They were cousins in a sense, because it was a polygamous marriage set up that they had, and unfortunately my father's dad died when he was still young, and so technically he and his siblings were then adopted by the eldest brother from the maiguru of my dad.

So he was like the doyen, He oversaw the family. For all intents and purposes, he was the "Sabhuku" of our village.

They built their homes in Seke communal area where they had

fields. It's about 500,000 hectares, which is the whole area that they resided in. They were very independent and interestingly, our great-grandfathers had actually emigrated from Zambia, so we are essentially "Tonga". Their ancestors moved from Zambia, crossed the Zambezi, and then settled in the Kadoma area. They, being Tongas, were very strong and very successful hunters, and they would hunt for animals, you know, kill them, and distribute, feed their families, and acquire wives and lands through that prowess which they had.

They were enterprising people. And so, when they moved to Kadoma, they settled in Kadoma in the Ngezi area and essentially, we are the Ngezi people, the Mupamombes so to speak. I must say all that rich heritage had a huge impact in my own life because the whole quest for independence, the whole quest for enterprise was very strong in them. Kadoma was a mining area, so there were gold fields, and so they acquired those gold fields by virtue of their strength and prowess, and after they had done that, then the Pioneer column came along, and it sought to strip them off their lands and eventually moved them to the tribal trust lands, and the story goes that my great-grandfathers, three of them, fought with the white men and were resisting being moved, and were ultimately killed on a hill in Kadoma because they were refusing to be moved by the white settlers who sought to move them. Ultimately, they were then forced to move as a clan with one surviving brother as the patriarch.

They went to the Seke area, and they befriended the chief Seke in that area who oversaw the whole area; Mambo Seke ruled between Goromonzi Epworth all the way through to Seke.

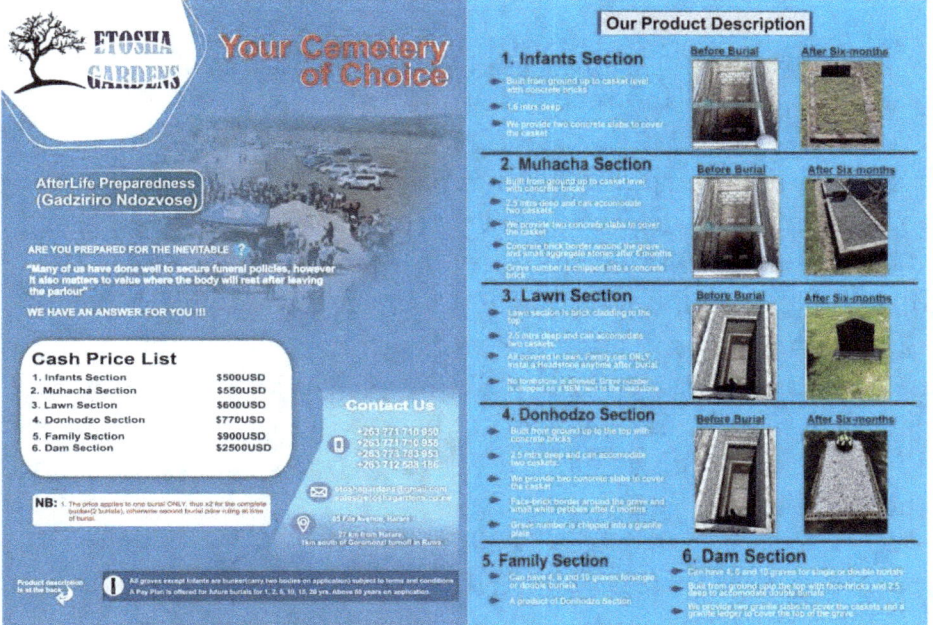

In Seke they were given a piece of land and they settled within that that area. They then intermarried and so forth. So that heritage, I guess, is part and parcel of me as a third-generation person.

Then, of course, being born in 1966, I was born into a family, that understood the politics of the day. They had very strong views. They supported the major political party of the day, ZANU-PF and funded it. As I mentioned earlier on, they were also active and particularly my dad, in Highfields paMachipisa, where the main shop was and that's what he oversaw, and they became very engaged in the community.

They were instrumental in helping set up the "Zimbabwe Grounds" sporting and recreational area; and my dad sponsored a soccer team called Black Hunters, which scouted for talent in the Highfields area. He sponsored that players like Shakeman Tauro who came through his hands and those are players that I watched as a kid when being taken to soccer to watch soccer at the Zimbabwe Grounds and ultimately, Gwanzura Stadium. My dad became very active in Chibuku soccer team and then ultimately, was also part and parcel of the founding of the Black Aces, which was the Highfields team. So, soccer became a major part of me, as did tennis, because there were also tennis courts that were set up at the Zimbabwe grounds.

So, I played tennis. My dad looked for a coach for me, it was none other than Much Masunda, who happened to be the brother of the secretary within their business. Gladys Masunda was the Personal Assistant (PA), and she served the brothers as a PA and her brother played tennis-the legendary Much Masunda, and ultimately, he became my tennis coach.

I must mention that I played tennis, and I played soccer because of the influence of my dad, and I became interested in business because of the influence of my dad. My dad, though, was not as educated as my mom was. He had received basic education and then undertook carpentry.

He then did a diploma in business at Ranch House College during the war when their business activities were reduced. My mom, on the other hand, as a state registered nurse, valued education, and she so desired that I get a good education. As a result, between them, they then decided that I would go to a multiracial school. I guess I can describe my generation as a relatively well-off, middle-class group of students that went to schools that were run as multiracial schools by the Dominican nuns.

I started school around 1972.

Interestingly, the Dominican Convent nuns had an influence in my life because I started off by going to Regina Mundi crèche, which was located on my street in Highfields. I remember I was amongst the first to go to crèche. We lived in old Highfields kuma Six Pounds, and I was sent to Regina Mundi crèche and that's where I cut my teeth in terms of education; while furthermore it also influenced my beliefs a Regina Mundi had a very strong Christian bias. We ourselves went to church every Sunday and my dad and mom are Methodists, and we used to go to old Highfields and sit on the floor with Ambuya Chogawho would discipline us if we were naughty, so we had to be attentive.

We would attend the church with the adults, but we sat on the floor out in the front. And so, the teaching was the same for adults and young children. So, at a very young age, I was indoctrinated into Christianity quite strongly, and then, of course, going to Regina Mundi was quite an experience. I wasn't the brightest kid, not in the least among my three siblings. I have a sister called Sandra Farai, now married to a Moyo, and she was a lot brighter than I was and I kind of struggled with that as a kid. But fortunately, my mum and dad were very aggressive and assertive with me, wanting me to always do my best and be top of the class, and that, I must say, I felt was a lot of pressure on me. I recall how whenever my sister exhibited more intelligence than me, she is being two years younger, it was traumatic for me. I then attended boarding school at a very young age.

I remember the day when my mum said: "you're going to boarding school", I thought Boarding was the name of the school. So, I was quite excited when they bought the uniform and all, but what I didn't quite understand was why they were buying blankets and sheets when at crèche, the blankets and sheets were already there. So, when my dad then drove me to Martindale Private School (which is some 80 kilometers away from Harare) and then left me there, I cried like a baby and hoped that he was going to come pick me up at five o'clock as usual, but he never did.

I remember how as it got dark on my first day at primary school with all strangers and nuns, and I sobbed away to sleep eventually. But I thought that they had abandoned me! Nevertheless, it was quite a process getting accustomed to boarding school life, and I eventually resigned to the fact that my parents didn't love me enough. I remember wondering if maybe I'd been a bad child, and if they had dumped me at this place. I mean, my mom didn't even come along when I was taken there. It was all too much for me. But the nuns were kind, and the senior boys were kind. I had made lots of friends. I remember fondly Tipawa Tagwirei, Honour Chikara, Patrick Dube, and others.

I befriended these guys as some came from Highfields, and so it was easier to relate to them. But we also had coloured kids in that multiracial society, and quite interestingly, its kind of, you know, opened my eyes to learning English. Eventually, at the end of the term, the Easter holiday arrived, and my dad came to pick me up. My goodness, I was so excited. I remember vividly that I was now going home, when in fact I had thought that boarding school was my new home.

So that was the life that I grew up in between 1972 and 1978. I was at boarding school for six years, and we had different teachers. I remember sister Madada, she was very strict in grade one, Sister Dorothy, less strict, more loving in grade two. Then we had a very tough master in standard one (in those days we did KG1 and KG2 before going to standard one and standard two and standard three and standard four). I also recall how that school had a great deal of discipline, so if you behaved badly, there was a male schoolteacher called Mr. Russo whop would see to it that all those who misbehaved were whacked and that disciplined us. In the boarding house we had the boarding mistress, a coloured lady by the name Mrs. Stewart, and her husband was the school keeper in terms of the foreman. He looked after the school property, all the electrics. He fixed things. He organized and managed the farm because it was a farm school. If ever any of us were naughty at boarding school, we were also whacked by Mr. Stewart. Even the nuns would whack us! There was one teacher in standard four, Sister Juanita, and she was a tough nun, I tell you, and she didn't brook any nonsense!

So, I grew up in that environment and that discipline really taught me to be a well-behaved kid. Interestingly, of course, there was also bullying, and we were bullied to great length because we had tuck. The seniors, in a sense, would toss us around, and consequently we would make sure we gave them some tuck for some protection. Ultimately, of course, at some point we became seniors ourselves, and in so doing, I remember very vividly (and I'm even embarrassed to say this) how I also became a bully at some point, until the school revolted against me, which taught me that bullying is not good. Another aspect of boarding school that I also remember was the fighting. I was also a fighter. I guess my dad had taught me to stand up for my rights at that primary school. I remember how in K G1 I had a punch-up with Honour Chikara! I also had a punch up with one of the toughest guys in the school; Kevin Dalmaida, who was also rated as one of the toughest guys in the school!

But you know, interestingly, after all these punch ups, these became some of my greatest friends. But I was one that didn't want to be bullied. I preferred being a bully myself. But the Honour Chikaras, the Kevin Dalmadias all became friends eventually. Another interesting aspect of boarding school life (being in the pre-independence years of the late 1970s) was that the war raged on stronger, but we remained at school.

Personally, I was fairly confused about politics at the time because the coloured guys that we went to school with, their parents or their dads were fighting for the Rhodesian army. The nuns were also terrified of the 'terrorists' and so there was a leaning at the school as most of the staff supported the Rhodesian Army. It was always strange to see Rhodesian soldiers when they came with the army trucks to visit their kids. Sometimes they would be passing along Bulawayo Road, and they would, take a turn to our school. We would see these army guys and in a sense, they were idolized. But then in contrast, when we went home for the holidays, we would be forced in a sense to listen to 'Radio Zimbabwe' which was broadcast from Mozambique and at 7 o'clock each evening, between 7:00 and 7:30 at night many black families were listening to the radio in Mozambique, where the likes of Webster, Shamu were on air, and my parents, you know, would be in support of vakomana.

As a result of this, I grew up a very confused kid because when I was at home, I was supporting vakomana, but when I was at school, I was supporting the Rhodesian Army, you know, in a sense, because of that dichotomy. It was only later at independence in 1980, when I moved to St. John's High School, Emerald Hill in Harare, that I started to understand nationalism. At that stage, independence had come, and I was now at school with the kids of Doctor Mazorodze who were steeped in understanding what the liberation struggle was all about. So, it was only at high school (circa 1980) that we knew now what independence meant.

This was now another multiracial school. That's when I began to inquire more and more from my dad, and his brothers about the struggle and, black empowerment, black determination Ultimately, I became reoriented politically, and that was a major transformation in my life because I then began to understand what life was all about. I began to understand what white privilege was all about and the economics of things, and I began to take an interest. At high school I studied French, I studied history, and that for me was for me, was my 'Age of Enlightenment'.
So, from 1979 to 1984 I was at St. John's High School. In my final year, I was made deputy head boy. At the school I played all sorts of sports.

We competed against the former white schools, and it was always fun to beat them to out-compete them, and show that we, although we had this underprivileged background' (relatively speaking) we still spoke good English, and we could take them head on and that's what we did. So, playing against the likes of Churchill, Vainona, Prince Edward brought for out the competitive edge within me, and I would compete assertively, to show that we as blacks were equally competent if not more competitive and could out-compete them on a level playing field. So, my schooling at St. John's High School, I transitioned from having been a head boy at Martindale primary school to now go on and be a sprogg or a skivvy in form-one, and this was also another major learning point for me. At St. John's, I was fortunate because I had an elder cousin, Elijah Junior Chanakirangoni, and he looked after me very well. I also then befriended guys like Farai Mazorodze and Adam Banda, and those guys really protected us. Even Wilberforce, Chaza, and some very big names. They've distinguished themselves now. Matthew, Gotora too - these seniors were our heroes because they understood life a whole lot more than us and them kind of looked after us.

In 1982, my uncle, Dr EJ Chanakira, was then appointed permanent secretary in the Ministry of Education. He had been educated in the USA during the struggle, and when he came back in 1980, he was made an Under Secretary in the Ministry of Education. He, along with my godfather, Dr Herbert Murewa, (who worked for the United Nations Development Program) really brought about an awareness because they served in government, and they brought an awareness of the need for public good, the need for equality, and one of the things that Doctor EJ advocated for was the abolishment of the 'Group A schools' and instead, he called for and instituted the truly multiracial schools, including the former 'Group A' schools, and he integrated blacks into them. At that time that was this was part and parcel of what the then Prime Minister Robert Mugabe wanted. So that transition was interesting for me because.

when I passed my O' levels, I then moved on to Churchill Boys High School, which at the time still had a limited number of blacks (the likes of Dominic, Mandizha and Farai Mazorodze) and I remember one incident when Farai literally drove away from the school after being bullied by white kids at Churchill.
He went home, and he took the gun belonging to one of his dad's bodyguards, and he brought it to school -Spencer Hostel, and literally threatened to shoot any white racists that would ill- treat him or any other black guy. He did it to make a point. So, you can see how at the time, racism was very strong. I remember the white guys would flush our heads down the loo if we did anything that challenged the superiority of the white guys. The whites didn't even want to shower with a black person... that's how rife racism was.

But we fought the system, and ultimately, I became the head boy at Spencer Hostel. I became a head boy at the school as well. As the first black head boy of Spencer Hostel, I did my best to make sure that there was equality and justice, although there were still some teachers who were racist. I remember getting 'six of the best', from one teacher because I had whacked a white boy. Churchill was a very sporty school, and personally, during my time at Churchill I swam, I played volleyball, I played soccer, and I earned my colours and wings in various sports, and that sort of approach to life kind of carried over through to varsity. At Churchill, I passed my matric, (we used to do matric in those days) I passed my matric very well, although I was interrupted by a trip to Libya, where we spent two months at the African Games while other people were at school. We went as the national basketball team and I tell you, although the experience was exhilarating, those two months cost me academically.

I think we were away for August and September, and I came back in October to study and then write exams in November. Surprisingly, I did relatively well (because I had carried my books to Libya, as I knew that otherwise I was supposed to be at school), but it really had a dent on my schooling, so much so that I almost flunked my A- levels. I got 4 points, and my parents and my uncle were very disappointed with my results. I personally was embarrassed because I was at the very least a B class student, y; I got 2 A's, 5 B's and 1C at O-levels. I got a 3, 4, 5 at metric and then at A- levels I got 2 D's and that was a huge disappointment and I flunked math's with a U and so with that near miss, my uncle Dr Chanakira wanted me to repeat my A-levels, but I thought that it was embarrassing to go back and repeat those A-levels, so I protested that proposal. I remember then going on to

Varsity, where we were labelled the so-called enlightened 'Ma-nose' brigade. The word 'Ma-nose' was coined at the University of Zimbabwe (UZ), and it was coined against us- the so-called 'black privilege' kids because we had gone to former white schools. Resultantly, we formed a soccer team, because in my first year, they would tease us saying, "you think that you are better than us", and they'd say "hatinga kundwi ne vanhu vano taura nemu minho" (we cannot be defeated by snobs).

Nevertheless, we went on to win the Vice Chancellors Cup with that team of ours called 'Ghostbusters 'in the third year. Again, it showed that resilient attitude that we had and that we didn't brook any tribalism, and we didn't brook any segregation because of the rich background that, for instance, I had obtained in my own life.

At the university, I registered for a Bachelor of Arts (BA) degree. Instead of what I had aspired for, which was either a Bachelor of Accounting (BAcc) or a Bachelor of Business Studies (BBS) or Computer Science.
So, with the points that I had, I could only make it into, without question, BA, even though most of my friends passed with better grades than I, and others flunked.

So, I humbly accepted my fate, registered for a BA degree (although there was a chance, I could qualify for one of the social science degrees). Eventually, I sweet-talked my way into a Bachelor of Science in Economics, even though there were various students with four points at A-levels who were competing for minimal slots. Nevertheless, after the interviews, I was fortunately one of the students who were accepted (courtesy of Rob Davis), and we started classes.

I remember thanking Professor Rob Davis and I said to him; "mark my words, you will, you won't regret why you admitted me as a special student"; and from then on, I became a totally different character. I focused on my studies throughout my first year, second year, and third year.

It was during those days that I met my girlfriend Caroline accidentally, after giving her a lift during my second year, (I had bought my first vehicle with funds saved up from the grant money that we would from the university, together with money that I saved up from holiday work). During vacations, I worked for my dad in his shops. I also got a job at the city of Harare, and I also later got a research job with Barclays Bank within the Small and Medium-sized Enterprises (SME) division, and this allowed me to accumulate some savings with which I bought myself a vehicle so that I could drive to varsity and leave varsity at my own time. I would always be amongst the last to leave the library; prior to that I had to take the school bus, which meant I had to leave the library at about 7:00pm or 8:00pm at the latest. But with my own vehicle, I could study as an undergraduate all the way up until 10:00pm, when the library closed.

So, I remember how after the library had closed, during one of those trips back home to Highfields that I met a lovely young lady who was hitch-hiking for a lift going to High Fields, and she was standing at the side of the road with a guy I knew- Andrew Chiduku, who apparently was courting her. So I went around the block, knowing that Andrew was standing at the lifts for High Fields when he lived in Mbare. So, I figured he was trying to escort the girl. So, I gave her a lift, and that is the Caroline that I'm married to; that's how I met my sweetheart, Caroline. That was during my second year in November, and we became friends first after that lift, and we began dating a couple of months later. Incidentally. She lived right next door to my best friend Raymond Ndlovhu in Highfeilds, and we had never seen this girl. Imagine! Caroline is my best friend, my confidant, and we were to get married in 1989.

Although I was still playing a bit of soccer, although I had a girlfriend, although I would party here and there, all in all, I was a really, really serious student focused on my work and therefore, it was no surprise when I graduated in the top six of my class with an upper second class degree, (I missed a first class graduation by three subjects). I had first class grades in economics, econometrics, and finance and banking. I had first class passes and upper second class passes in those subjects.

So, getting a job from there was relatively easy because, the banks would take the top graduates and the Reserve Bank would take only upper second class passes preferably; so, if you got an upper second-class degree, you were guaranteed a job at the central bank. So, I ended up at the central bank in 1988 and because of those grades, I was automatically accepted onto the master's program. So, I did my master's on a part-time basis whilst I was working at the Reserve Bank of Zimbabwe in the Public Finance and Economics division of the Central Bank. I worked very well there. I was recognized, (although I was a rookie young junior economist) so much that even the chief economist, Sam Malaba, liked the work that I did. I was into quantitative economics. I did research and was responsible for the Public Finance Section Bulletin of the Reserve Bank. I always went the extra mile in my work so that my reports were always well-informed.

I worked at the Central bank and did my part-time, between 1988 and 1990, when I then completed my masters.

Caroline and I got pregnant in 1989 and so on the 1st of April of that year, I married her in court, and started a new job at Bard Discount House. So, I left the Reserve Bank to join Bard Discount House as an investment analyst. This job I got was as a Trainee Investment Analyst and I desired this job.
I must mention that prior to this job, I had discovered from my research on the market that the best banker in Zimbabwe at the

time was a guy called Charles Gurney. I managed to discover this because as part of my responsibility within the Reserve Bank bulletin, I'd be interviewing all the CEOs of the banks and I found this gentleman Charles Gurney to be insightful, so much that when Bard Discount House advertised for a job, I knew it was an opportunity to work for the smartest banker in town and I applied instantly.

I remember how there were 400 applicants, and yours truly made it through the three rounds, and I got appointed to be a Trainee Investment Analyst, and that was my change in career.

from being a professional economist to being trained as a fund manager. So, I worked there for two years and then became the youngest ever director in a registered financial institution when Bard Investment Services appointed me a director at the age of 24. I remember how in my job I was very aggressive. After all, Caroline was pregnant, and I needed to do everything to cater for my growing family. I remember my dad saying to me: "your girlfriend's pregnant, asi une chii mfana iwewe? You don't even own a bed!"

The only things that I owned at the time were my car, a Renault 12, and my suits, because that's all I would buy. I wanted to look very smart, so I'd buy clothes and then spend my money, and so my dad knew that because I was being subsidized by him somewhat.

That led me to me sitting down in Highfields where I remember doing my first goal planning list. I sat down and resolved on the things that I wanted to achieve in my life. I needed a better job. I needed to buy a bed. I needed to have my own house to rent and to prepare for the coming child- Panashe Panuel Chanakira. So, the job at Bard Discount House was a godsend because it then put me on a good path for five years. I got trained to be an investment banker, I got the directorship at age 24. They then promoted me into the dealing room, and I became what they call a GILT dealer - those are government stocks- and I ran that desk for them.

I made them a lot of money; I remember one deal; I made them a million U.S. dollars plus. That was the biggest deal that they had ever done. I knew I was a deal maker; notwithstanding that these guys had trained me, they had exposed me, they even sent me to London, and they sent me to South Africa. I knew that I was getting the best exposure possible.

Five years later, my friend Tsitsi Masiywa (who was always a friend at Varsity) invited me to Empretec because she knew from Varsity that I had this dream to start my own bank. And so, I went to Empretec, and got entrepreneurial training. AT Empretec they teach the 10 attributes for becoming a successful entrepreneur, and that was the genesis of Kingdom Financial Kingdom Securities Holdings Limited (KFKSHL), because after I attended that course in May 1994, I then wrote my business plan for KFKSHL and then resigned from my job in October 1994 to set up Kingdom Securities Trading.

Fortunately, I had acquired the experience, I had the exposure and at that time I was inspired by Nick Vengerai and Gibson Gwendai who were the first Blacks to form independent financial banking institutions; those guys were my seniors at Bard Discount House, and they became a benchmark of sorts.

I could watch what they had done, Nick and Gibson formed the third one, Intermarket Bank and I tried to join them, but to no avail. Then I rushed over to them Never Mlhanga and asked requested to join his team, but they felt that they had enough guys. There were already four, if not five partners in their entity, and so I couldn't join them.

So, since I couldn't join them, I thought, "what the heck," I may as well start my own. Consequently, I got together with the stockbroker, Solomon Mugavazi, a corporate banker, a chartered accountant, Lucia Sibanda and then my junior at Bard Discount house called Franky Kufa, who was a superior money market dealer. So, I said: "guys, let's form this".

I wrote out the business plan using the Empretech Business model and quit my job. I recall how I was sent on garden and leave for three months between October, November, and December, and on the 1st of December we started an informal unregistered discount house operation while we were waiting for our Reserve Bank license which was eventually issued in August 1995, and we became a formally registered discount house, thereby becoming the first discount house in Zimbabwe's banking sector.

Let me also tell you why I chose the name Kingdom for my bank.

At marriage, the driving factor for me, was provision of a good livelihood for my family. Fortunately, I was able to get a housing loan (as I was a director at Bard Discount House), so I bought my first house. In Cranborne. I also had an executive company car.

But the moment I quit; it meant all those privileges would be gone, and I still had to pay off my housing loan... notwithstanding the fact that I'd moved from Cranborne to an executive house in Eastlea.

So, to start KFKSHL I had to sell my assets since I had no capital. I also started working part-time as a lecturer, on top of another side hustle which saw me going to auctions, buying, and selling and re-upholstering furniture, and then after a while I was doing it with cars. All the while I was saving up capital for this dream that I had of starting a bank, but unfortunately, in the process, I had a car accident that resulted in the death of a child. The child was the same age as my own little son, Panashe, and that experience was devastating to me.

It was that experience that led me to do away with boozing, because at the time, I used to play 'boozers' soccer, and although I was a responsible adult, I would drink socially. Nevertheless, on the day that accident happened, I had had two beers. Resultantly it became a police case, and I was tried for culpable homicide and fortunately, by the grace of God, I was acquitted. Nonetheless, that was a major turning point in my life.

Although I had been raised as a Christian Methodist, and although I had gone to Catholic schools, till, that adversity made me call out the God saying: "Lord, if only you could save this child, I promise you, Lord, if you save this child, I'll reform!"
Unfortunately, the child died in my hands, and it was such a painful experience that it became a Damascus moment for me. So, I then surrendered my life to completely Christ; and began attending the church where my wife had already been going to:

African Faith Mission (AFM), a Pentecostal church. I recall how the pastor could see that I was quite badly affected by this death.

Fortunately, the parents of this child were very understanding, and they forgave me, particularly the father who was in prison at that time, and I really felt terrible, thinking to myself: "what if that had happened to me or my child?" As I had two kids.
That's when I made a conscious decision that I was never going to touch a beer again, and that was the last beer I had. I then surrendered my life to Christ and a month later, I got baptized in the AFM church as a born again Christian, and so I began to search the scriptures, looking for what life meant, and while doing so, I came across what became my favourite scripture: Matthew 6, verse 33; "Seek ye first Kingdom of God and his righteousness, and all these things shall be added unto you".

That became a key scripture for me. Furthermore, at the time, Amon Chinyemba was my wise pastor, and I remember on one occasion when how he came and prayed for me, he read this scripture, Proverbs 31 versus 1-6;

The Words of King Lemuel
31 The words of King Lemuel. An oracle that his mother taught him:
2 What are you doing, my son? What are you doing, son of my womb?
What are you doing, son of my vows?
3 Do not give your strength to women, your ways to those who destroy kings.
4 It is not for kings, O Lemuel, it is not for kings to drink wine, or for rulers to take strong drink,

5 lest they drink and forget what has been decreed and pervert the rights of all the afflicted.
6 Give strong drink to the one who is perishing, and wine to those in bitter distress.

These verses talk of a good king whose name is Lemuel. The king's mother recites those instructions, and I always felt I was a king. Remember, I'm from the Mupamombe clan and I always knew that I am royal blood, I am blue-blooded. So, when then this pastor who didn't even know that I was royalty happened to pick that scripture, it was touching to me. Also, ironically, my dad's name is Lemuel. I had even named my son Panache Lamuel Chanakira, in honour of my dad, and therefore the genesis of Kingdom is in those scriptures, "Seek ye first the Kingdom of God and his righteousness, and all these things shall be added unto you," and the Proverbs 31:1-6, the scripture the pastor quoted when he laid hands on me.
So, Kingdom became the name, with the crown as the logo.

Let me conclude by stating that I would really like to see the socio-economic renaissance of Zimbabwe soon. I feel that to do so, and if the younger generations are to attain the type of lifestyles that we lived and were privileged to experience, I believe that there are certain steps that need to be taken.

Firstly, let me mention that I have become a very active member of our economic society. Currently, I'm the president of the Zimbabwe Economic Society. I'm also a member of an organization called 'Network 58', where we espouse the visions of what we would want to see for our country, and a key part of what we do is identify what has gone wrong.

To date, we've been able to review a lot of the policies that have been put in situ, and consequently we also discuss solutions for our economy because, at the end of the day, if we do not sort out our economy, and concurrently if we don't sort out our politics, then we are going nowhere fast and that troubles and worries me very much.

Resultantly, a major driver of the values that I've adopted within Network 58 is that we want a yield of **R.A.D.I.C.A.L** Zimbabweans; where **R.A.D.I.C.A.L** stands for:
Respect, **A**ccountability, **D**iscipline, **I**ntegrity, **C**ourage, **A**ttitude and **L**ove.
I genuinely believe that if we espouse those values. We can transform this nation.